TEN UNIVERSAL PRINCIPLES

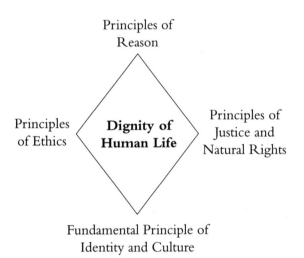

Principles of
Reason

Principles
of Ethics

**Dignity of
Human Life**

Principles of
Justice and
Natural Rights

Fundamental Principle of
Identity and Culture

ROBERT J. SPITZER, S.J., PH.D.

TEN UNIVERSAL PRINCIPLES

*A Brief Philosophy of
the Life Issues*

IGNATIUS PRESS   SAN FRANCISCO

Nihil Obstat: David Leigh, S.J.
October 28, 2009

Imprimatur: † Most Reverend Tod D. Brown
Bishop of Orange, California
April 29, 2011

Cover art:
Background photograph of pillar © iStockphoto.com

School of Athens (detail of Plato and Aristotle)
Raphael (1483–1520)
Stanza della Segnatura, Stanze di Raffaello,
Vatican Palace
Scala/Art Resource, New York

Cover design by John Herreid

In memory of Father Thomas King, S.J.,
who dedicated himself courageously in the academy to the
the intrinsic dignity of every human being,
and to Camille Pauley,
who has dedicated her life to healing the culture
through the ten principles in this book.

CONTENTS

ACKNOWLEDGMENTS

My sincere appreciation and thanks go to Camille Pauley, who, once again, has contributed so much of her time and energy bringing this book to light. I want to thank her for the hours spent in typing it, and the fine editorial suggestions made for our common mission. My thanks to Joan Jacoby for her work and help in the final edition of this book.

I would also like to thank the many people who have supported the creation of an intellectual statement for the life issues throughout the years, particularly Joseph Koterski, S.J.; Sean Raftis, S.J.; Kenneth VanDerhoef; Eileen Geller; Dan Kennedy; Michael Pauley; Dirk Bartram; Rich Thrasher; Joe Wetzel; Aloysius and Jody Mullally; Bob and Liz Crnkovich; James and Doris Cassan; Lisa-Ann Oliver; Francis Beckwith; members of University Faculty for Life; members of Legatus; and the many other supporters of this movement.

INTRODUCTION

The evolution of culture and civilization has arisen out of the development of ten fundamental principles. Three of them concern evidence and objective truth, three of them concern ethics, three of them concern the dignity and treatment of human beings within civil society, and one of them concerns personal identity and culture. Failure to teach and practice any one of these principles can lead to an underestimation of human dignity, a decline in culture, the abuse of individuals and even groups of individuals, and an underestimation of ourselves and our potential in life. Failure to teach and practice *several* of these principles will most *certainly* lead to widespread abuse and a general decline in culture.

This assertion is not made arbitrarily or out of a so-called slippery slope argument, for history is so replete with examples of these failures and their consequences that it would be wholly unreasonable and irresponsible *not* to infer its validity. We have all heard the cliché attributed to Einstein, that "insanity is doing the same thing over and over and expecting different results." Our[1] objective then in presenting this curriculum is first and foremost to prevent great harm to individuals and communities, and thereby to prevent this kind

---

[1] "Our" refers to the many colleagues who help me to proliferate these principles through educational organizations (such as Healing the Culture) and institutes of scholarly research (such as University Faculty for Life). The missions of these organizations and their contact information are given on the final pages of this book.

of "insanity" from repeating itself in our national and even international history.

A brief review of these principles will give further credence to our claim that they are an essential safeguard of human dignity, welfare, and community. Some may say that it is the legal system or democracy or the courts that are the real protectors of individuals, culture, and society; but as will become evident, without the ten principles, democracy could vote out the rights of human beings, court systems could legalize every form of indignity and harm, and legal systems would have nothing upon which to base their laws. Again, one does not have to look very far to see these abuses in world history with its kangaroo courts, arbitrary marginalization and persecution of peoples, and justification of slavery, discrimination, and maltreatment. Systems and courts are mere structures. They are designed to operationalize something beyond themselves. That "something", we would maintain, is the fruit—the best fruit of the human spirit that we believe to be enshrined in these ten principles.

TEN UNIVERSAL PRINCIPLES:
A Brief Philosophy of the Life Issues

The following ten universal principles form the foundation of civility, justice, and objectivity in cultures throughout the world. Their presence assures the possibility of humane civilization and their absence (even their partial absence) opens the path for corruption, deceit, injustice, and cultural decline. Three principles concern objectively verifiable truth, three concern personal ethics and virtue, three concern political justice and rights, and one concerns the development of great culture.

I. Principles of Reason

Principle 1: The Principle of Complete Explanation (Socrates, Plato, and Aristotle)
The best opinion or theory is the one that explains the most data.

Principle 2: The Principle of Noncontradiction (Plato and Aristotle)
Valid opinions or theories have no internal contradictions.
Classical formulation: A real being cannot both be and not be the same thing, in the same respect, at the same place and time.

Principle 3: The Principle of Objective Evidence (Plato and Aristotle)
Nonarbitrary opinions or theories are based upon publicly verifiable evidence.

II. Principles of Ethics

Principle 4: The Principle of Nonmaleficence (Jesus, Moses, and worldwide religious traditions)
Avoid unnecessary harms; if a harm is unavoidable, minimize it.
Silver Rule: Do *not* do unto others what you would *not* have them do unto you.

Principle 5: The Principle of Consistent Ends and Means (Augustine)
The end does not justify the means.

Principle 6: The Principle of Full Human Potential (Las Casas)
Every human being (or group of human beings) deserves to be valued according to the full level of human development, not according to the level of development currently achieved.

III. Principles of Justice and Natural Rights

Principle 7: The Principle of Natural Rights (Suarez, Locke, Jefferson, and Paine)
All human beings possess in themselves (by virtue of their existence alone) the inalienable rights of life, liberty, and property ownership; no government gives these rights, and no government can take them away.

Principle 8: The Principle of the Fundamentality of Rights (Suarez, Locke, and Jefferson)
The more fundamental right is the one which is necessary for the possibility of the other; where there is a conflict, we should resolve in favor of the more fundamental right.

Principle 9: The Principle of Limits to Freedom (Locke and Montesquieu)
One person's (or group's) freedoms cannot impose undue burdens upon other persons (or groups).

IV. Fundamental Principle of Identity and Culture

Principle 10: The Principle of Beneficence (Jesus)
Aim at optimal contribution to others and society.
The Golden Rule: Do unto others as you would have them do unto you.

I.

PRINCIPLES OF REASON

Our first three principles concern the validation of truth claims. No bias, ostracization, marginalization, or persecution ever occurred without someone claiming that their biases were the "truth". Nazi propaganda began with the assertion that Jewish people, Gypsies, and others were *really* inferior. Stalinist propaganda began with claims that non-Communists are *really* dissidents and troublemakers. The Khmer Rouge's propaganda began with claims that educated urbanites were *really* undermining the common good. Even our Supreme Court advocated that black people were *really* inferior to whites such that their liberty rights were subordinated to white people's property rights. The word "really" is a code word for "truth". We attribute a kind of sanctity to the word "truth" and allow it to ground our fundamental beliefs about the meaning and purpose of life, the dignity of human beings, and the goodness of culture. It has so much implicit power that we must be very careful about how we use it, and very precise about how we might establish its presence.

The following three principles were formally set out by Socrates, Plato, and Aristotle twenty-four hundred years ago in response to arguments originally formulated by the Sophists.[1] They still remain with us today because the failure to

---

[1] Today, "sophistry" means the practice of formulating confusing or illogical arguments with the intention of deceit. Plato believed that the Sophists

teach and practice them results in sophistry, skepticism,[2] and cynicism[3]—three cultural viewpoints that are indifferent to the truth, and have, on many occasions, led to the undermining of human dignity and community.

Let us briefly examine Skepticism, which ironically first arose in Plato's Academy. It emphasized one aspect of Sophism—namely, the dubitable and unfounded truth value of every assertion. Recall that Sophists were devoted to relativity of the truth (all opinions are equally valid), which entailed making weaker arguments seem stronger (making dubious claims seem reasonably valid) and making stronger arguments seem weaker (making reasonably validated claims seem dubious). The Skeptics made the latter a habitual practice, which later had the effect of making any truth claim seem unfounded or unreasonable. Though technically every truth claim can be doubted, it does not mean that it is unfounded and unreasonable. If one assumes the invalidity

---

were attempting to promote relativity of the truth, i.e., that all opinions are equally valid. In order to combat this, he set out in many of his *Dialogues* a methodology that would help to decide objectively which arguments were stronger and which ones weaker. His student Aristotle formalized this in what we today call "logic" and "rules of evidence" (see Aristotle's *Prior Analytics*).

[2] Skepticism was originally formulated by certain Sophists, but became a school of thought (ironically) in Plato's Academy after the death of Aristotle in the first century B.C. by Aenesidemus.

[3] Cynicism was a school of thought initiated by Antisthenes (a student of Socrates) in about the fourth century B.C. The Cynics rejected convention (e.g., religion, manners, and dress), in order to pursue a simple lifestyle. By the nineteenth century, "cynicism" came to mean not only rejection of convention, but also rejection of anything accepted as good, certain, or true, giving rise to a mentality of jadedness and negativity, which scorned most beliefs and ideals. Though Plato and Aristotle did not encounter these thoughts as doctrines of the Cynics, they did encounter them among certain Sophists and Skeptics. Their response was to develop an objective methodology for determining not only what assertions could be shown to be invalid or false, but also what assertions could be known as true.

of all truth claims, it creates a despair of the truth, which means that its proponents are not responsible for validating anything. Once one is relieved of the responsibility of validating a claim (because all such validation is assumed to be futile), then one can hold absolutely anything with impunity—"Life is brutish, ugly, and short" is just as true as "Life contains the potential for purpose, goodness, and love." "Human beings are nothing more than mere chemicals" is just as true as "Human beings manifest activities that go beyond the laws of physics and chemistry." The assumption that truth can never be reached makes all incomplete, arbitrary (merely subjective), and even illogical claims seem just as true as claims that are logical, grounded in objective evidence (nonarbitrary), and more complete (explain more data). This practice could lead to an underestimation of human potential and dignity, and thereby to a decline in cultural ideals and the striving to create a better world.

Many of us have heard the expression "arbitrarily asserted, arbitrarily denied"—that is, if you assert a claim without evidence, it can just as easily be denied without evidence. Plato and Aristotle recognized that all opinions are not equally valid. Einstein's theory of the universe is better than Newton's theory of the universe. Modern mathematics is superior to Euclidian mathematics. Jeffersonian political philosophy is superior to fascist political philosophy. Martin Luther King's ethical practice was superior to Hitler's ethical practice. Even though such claims may seem intuitively obvious, we must be able to establish these facts; otherwise they are simply arbitrarily asserted (and therefore can be arbitrarily denied).

Let me illustrate this with a typical scenario from my introductory philosophy classes. Year after year, I begin with the simple question that originates with Plato, namely, "How many of you believe that all opinions have validity and should be respected?" More than 50% of the class will respond in the affirmative because they want to respect their fellow human beings. This good intention leads them to confuse the goodness of human beings with the goodness of their opinions, which prevents them from asking whether the *opinion* (apart from the good human being who uttered it) is respectable in its own right. After seeing the show of hands, I ask, "Well, then, do you think that Hitler's opinion about genocide is valid and should be respected?" "Do you think that the Supreme Court's opinion about the inferiority of black people in the *Dred Scott* decision is valid and should be respected?" They all respond, "Of course not—but those are really obvious examples." I tell them afterward, "Yes, but it shows something—that even though you want to respect the *person* who is asserting an opinion, you must be careful about respecting the *content* of that opinion. The content of an opinion might be invalid and even unworthy of respect." This, of course, engenders the question: "All right, so how do you distinguish between the content of a good opinion and the content of a bad opinion?" and I respond, "I'm glad you asked that question." The brief answer is as follows.

There are three important methods for ascertaining the validity of an opinion: (1) the *quantity* of evidence (see Principle 1, the principle of most complete explanation), (2) the *logical consistency* of arguments (see Principle 2, the principle of noncontradiction), and (3) the *quality* of evidence (see Principle 3, the principle of objective evidence—the public verifiability of evidence). The general rule is this: if an opinion explains more data, is based on objective (publicly verifiable) evidence, and has no internal contradictions, it is better (truer) than an opinion that explains less data, has merely subjective (arbitrary) evidence, and has internal contradictions. I find that very few students challenge the idea of truer claims explaining more data or truer claims being based on objective (publicly verifiable) evidence. However, I occasionally meet a student who will attempt to challenge the principle of noncontradiction; I usually counter (successfully) with Aristotle's astute defense of it (see below, Principle 2). Let us proceed to an explanation of these three principles.

Principle 1: The Principle of Complete Explanation

The best opinion or theory is the one that explains the most data.

The general principle is this: opinions that explain the most data and are verified by the most evidence are better than those that do not. The vast majority of people consider this principle to be self-evident because if greater explanatory power and more evidence is not better, then additional evidence and explanatory power add nothing, which means that all evidence and explanatory power are essentially worthless. This leaves us with only our subjective assertions, which most people do not consider to be good enough.

For example, as suggested previously, Einstein's theory about the universe is better than Newton's theory because it explains more data. (Newton was unaware of most of the data that the special and general theories of relativity account for.) Again, calculus has more explanatory power than algebra and trigonometry because it can account for curves through derivative and integral functions, which algebra and trigonometry cannot do on their own. This applies to virtually every science and social science. The more data a theory or hypothesis explains, the better it is.

With respect to life issues, this principle is important because a theory of human personhood that treats a person as a mere individual physical thing (materialism) does not explain the data of persons being self-conscious or having transcendental desires (such as the desire for complete and unconditional Truth, Love, Goodness, Beauty, and Being). Therefore, materialism's explanation of many acknowledged human powers and activities, such as empathy, *agape* (self-sacrificial love), self-consciousness, the desire for integrity and virtue, the sense of the spiritual, and the drive for self-transcendence, is, at best, weak. Theories that attempt to account for and explain these data, such as hylomorphism or transmaterialism, should be preferred to ones that do not, such as biological reductionism, materialism, and behaviorism.[4]

The underestimation of human personhood can lead to the underliving of one's life; for if one does not think one has a spiritual dimension, one may not pay attention to spiritual desires. If one does not think of oneself as having a conscience, one will not attempt to listen to it. If one thinks that love is merely a biochemical reaction, one is not likely to make it a priority, particularly if it should require self-sacrifice. Evidently, this one "little" assumption (the underestimation of personhood in materialism) could radically alter the character of one's life, relationships, purpose, and pursuits.

---

[4] It is not surprising, for example, that B. F. Skinner's behavioristic work, which attempts to explain all human activities in terms of stimulus-response reactions to one's surrounding environment, is entitled *Beyond Freedom and Dignity* (Indianapolis: Hackett Publishing, 2002). A behavioristic system cannot begin to explain either freedom or dignity, because it cannot get outside of its materialistic assumptions that necessarily preclude empathy, the pursuit of genuine love, self-consciousness, the desire for integrity and virtue, the sense of the spiritual, and the drive for self-transcendence.

There is another more serious consequence of the under-estimation of human personhood, namely, the undervaluation of real people. If we consider human beings to be mere matter without the self-possession necessary for freedom and love, without unique lovability, or without spiritual or transcendent significance, we might view human beings as mere "things". If humans are viewed as mere things, then they can be treated as mere things, and this assumption has led historically to every form of human tragedy. Human beings might be thought of as slaves, cannon fodder, tools for someone else's well-being, subjects for experimentation, or any number of other indignities and cruelties that have resulted from human "thingification".

The principle of most complete explanation has a well-known corollary, namely, "There are far more errors of omission than commission", which means that leaving out data is just as harmful to the pursuit of truth as getting the wrong data or making logical errors. This adage is related to the moral saying that "there are far more *sins* of omission than commission." In the case of the underestimation of human personhood, history has revealed how close the relationship between errors and sins truly is.

Principle 2: The Principle of Noncontradiction

Valid opinions or theories have no internal contradictions.

Classical formulation: A real being cannot both be and not be the same thing, in the same respect, at the same place and time.

This principle goes back to the time of Plato and was formally stated by Aristotle. It is *the* most fundamental principle in logic (and, therefore, the most important principle for proving anything). It may be stated as follows: "For any real or imaginary being X, X cannot be both A and not-A in the same respect at the same place and time." For example, I cannot be both six feet and not six feet in the same respect at the same place and time. This computer cannot be both the shape of a square and not the shape of a square in the same respect at the same place and time. Furthermore, I can't even *think* of a computer being in the shape of a square and not in the shape of a square in the same respect at the same place and time.[5]

Since contradictions can never be real and can never be thought, we want to avoid them in any good logical argument, because we know that when they occur, they must be *false*. Thus, we don't want to say that a square-circle exists in the same respect at the same place and time, because a circle is a nonsquare (it does not have four inscribed right angles). If I said that a square-circle exists, it would be the same thing as saying that a square-nonsquare exists, which you and everyone else can't even think of. Similarly, it would be equally absurd to assert that a proton-electron existed, because an electron acts in precisely the opposite fashion of a proton with respect to its charge (that is, when protons attract, electrons repel; and when protons repel, electrons attract). Thus, to assert that a proton-electron exists is the same thing as asserting that a proton-nonproton exists in the same respect at the same place and time. This we can all recognize to be false.

Every once in a while a student will try to say, "How do you know that the principle of noncontradiction is correct?" And I simply give him Aristotle's response in book 4 (chapters 3 and 4) of the *Metaphysics*. In that work, Aristotle

---

[5] For examples of this, see Aristotle, *Metaphysics*, bk. 4, chap. 4.

toys with people who are uncertain about the principle of noncontradiction, by pushing them to silence and the status of a vegetable, because every claim they make would have to be meaningless. He reasons that if contradictory claims are just as valid as noncontradictory claims, then all words and all claims are meaningless.[6]

The denial of the principle of noncontradiction leads to the absurdity that everything is both X and not-X in the same respect at the same time and is also neither X nor not-X at the same place and time. This means that all sentences and all words are absolutely meaningless.[7] One cannot even *think* of anything meaningful within one's own mind. This reduces every opponent of the principle of noncontradiction to the status of a vegetable.

The principle of noncontradiction comes up frequently with respect to pro-life issues. For example, some courts say that human embryos have rights of inheritance and can sue after birth for pre-birth injuries (meaning that human embryos are persons with rights),[8] while other courts declare that human embryos are not persons and do not have even the right to life,[9] which is an obvious contradiction. Again, some biologists hold at once that a single-celled human zygote has a full human genome (and therefore cannot be considered anything other than a human being), and then claim that if the single-celled human zygote is not implanted, it is not yet a human being—another inherent contradiction.

Again, some people hold that freedom is both "getting what I want when I want it" and also "being able to live for what is most pervasive, enduring, deep". Now, the first

---

[6] Ibid., bk. 4, chap. 3, 1006a30–1008a10.

[7] Ibid., bk. 4, chap. 3, 1006a15 *ff.*

[8] See the court cases in note 5, p. 19 below.

[9] See *Roe v. Wade*, 410 U.S. 113 (1973), Sec. IX.A. Hereinafter, all section numbers will be given in the text rather than in a footnote.

definition of freedom is frequently antithetical to commitment (because commitment might mean delaying or refusing what I want right now), while the second definition of freedom must be consistent with commitment (because getting to what is most pervasive, enduring, and deep may require "stick-to-itness" over the long term). Thus, it would be a contradiction to assert that both definitions of freedom can be true in the same respect at the same place and time.

Principle 3: The Principle of Objective Evidence

Nonarbitrary opinions or theories are based upon publicly verifiable evidence.

The best kind of evidence is that which is accessible to everyone. This is not to say that my private religious experience or my private awareness of self is not real or true, but it is only accessible to me, and so it is not good evidence to be used to prove something publicly. When something is only accessible to me, it is called "subjective", but when something is accessible to everyone, it is called "objective".

There are two kinds of evidence that are considered to be publicly accessible: (1) a posteriori evidence (sensorial evidence) and (2) a priori evidence (evidence from necessity).

A posteriori evidence is empirical evidence, that is, evidence that is accessible to our five senses. The vast majority of us with normal sensorial acuity view this kind of evidence as publicly verifiable because it is almost universally publicly accessible. To say that I have a pen in my hand can be verified by everyone in the room who has normal visual acuity. To say that I am speaking out loud can be verified by everyone in the room who has normal auditory acuity.

Instruments of measurement can extend the range of a posteriori evidence, because these instruments can probe and measure the empirical world in ways that are not *directly* accessible to our senses; yet the readings on our instruments can be publicly corroborated by anyone who has normal visual acuity. For example, three of us can be looking at three thermometers in this room and agree that it is seventy-two degrees Fahrenheit right now.

A priori evidence is based on the principle of noncontradiction (see Principle 2 above) and is the basis for mathematical, logical, and metaphysical truths. It holds that any contradictory state of affairs is impossible (and therefore can never be real). For example, a square-circle of the same area at the same place and time can never be real because the corners of a square cannot coincide with the absence of corners in a circle in the same respect at the same place and time. Similarly, proton-electrons cannot exist in the same respect, at the same place and time, because a particle like an electron, which repels other electrons, cannot coincide with a particle like a proton, which attracts electrons, in the same respect at the same place and time. The same holds true for a so-called wavicle (something that acts like a wave and particle in the same respect at the same place and time). Waves are diffuse and spread out while particles are self-enclosed and collide; and nature cannot have a self-enclosed, spreading-out reality in the same respect at the same place and time.

Yet, contradictions can tell us more. In some cases, the opposite of a contradictory proposition can tell us something that must be *true*. For example, if we can show that the proposition "Past time is infinite" is a contradiction, then we will know that it is impossible for past time to be infinite. But if past time cannot be infinite, then it must be finite. So the contradiction in the proposition "Past time is infinite" also tells us that the opposite proposition "Past time is finite" is true. Similarly, if we can prove that it is contradictory to assert that an unconditioned Being (God) is material (conditioned by space and time), then we know that the proposition "God is material" is false; but this means that the proposition "God is immaterial" (transcends space-time) must be true.

Now let us return to our point, namely, that if we want to prove something to somebody, we have to use evidence that is either a posteriori, or a priori, or a combination of both, because these two kinds of evidence are publicly verifiable (that is, they can be verified by anyone who has normal sensorial and intellectual acuity). We cannot simply assert something as a matter of our *subjective* opinion (that is, an opinion that we *claim* to be true just because we felt or believed that it was so). This would be merely subjective verification, and, therefore, it could not be used to *prove* something to somebody else.

With respect to the pro-life movement, Dr. Jerome Lejeune showed that a single-celled human zygote (even if it is not implanted) has a full human genome. The presence of the full human genome *in a zygote* (the initial cell formed when a *new* organism is produced by sexual reproduction) will ordinarily become a fully actualized human being if he encounters no natural or artificial impediment in the development process.

It should be noted that the presence of a full human genome alone does not constitute a human being, for a full human genome may be present in any somatic cell in a human body. A somatic cell is any cell making up an organism, such as a skin cell or a bone cell, which is distinguished from a zygote, formed by germline cells constituting a new, actualizable human being. A bone cell or a skin cell will not develop into a full human being, but the presence of a full human genome *in a zygote* (the initial cell produced when a new organism is formed by sexual reproduction) will ordinarily result in a fully actualized unique human being in the absence of natural or artificial impediments. For this reason, Dr. Lejeune considered a human zygote (implanted or not implanted) to be a human being.

He was able to show this through public verification, through an instrument called a DNA sequencer (a posteriori evidence). Any person who wanted to verify this fact could use his sequencer or another sequencer to establish the same result. Therefore, he claimed *objectively* that a single-celled human zygote was a human being. He then went on to use the same instrument to establish that the single-celled human zygote had genetic material from both the mother and father but was a very different being from both the mother and the father because of the genetic combination. Once again, anyone who wanted to use his sequencer or another sequencer could establish the same fact objectively. He then claimed that, under normal conditions, this single-celled human zygote would develop into a unique, fully actualized human being on the basis of the genetic code present in the single-celled human zygote. Again, anyone who possessed similar DNA sequencers could establish this same fact. This enabled him to conclude that there was not only a unique human being present at the stage of a single-celled zygote, but also a unique human being that would become fully actualized in the vast majority of cases. Given this, we can say that if persons are defined as actualiz*able* human beings, then a single-celled human zygote would have to be considered a person.

Notice that if we do not use "actualiz*able*" in our definition of "person", then any human being which is not fully actualized could be considered a nonperson. That would present a problem because it is very difficult to establish the point at which a human being is fully actualized. From a strictly biological point of view, it would seem to be when full brain, bone, tissue, and muscular development has taken place, which would seem to be somewhere between the ages of twelve and twenty-two (depending on the particular human being). Furthermore, after the age of twenty-two, one begins to lose some of the full actualization reached at the age of twenty-two. Therefore, "full actualization" can never be used as a criterion for human personhood, because it is quite arbitrary. Needless to say, partial actualization would also be quite arbitrary, because who is to say what part of actualization suddenly makes a human being a person? (Would it be 30%? 40%? 50%? It would all depend on a *subjective* preference.)

So how can we get to an *objective* (nonarbitrary, publicly verifiable) definition of human personhood? We have to remove everything that is arbitrary. But if we remove everything that is arbitrary, such as stage of development, full actualization, etc., we are left with only one nonarbitrary criterion for "person", namely, the presence of a human being; that is, the presence of a full human genome in a human organism, which, in the vast majority of cases, can be expected to become fully actualized. At the earliest stage of development, this human being is a one-celled human zygote, even if it is not implanted.

In *Roe v. Wade*, the majority rendered its decision that fetuses in the first and second trimesters (and, in a qualified way, in the third trimester) were *not* persons on the basis of its inability to find consensus among randomly selected experts. It even failed to establish a *subjective* criterion (let alone an objective one), because *non*consensus among arbitrarily chosen experts does not prove anything; it is the absence of evidence.

After Dr. Lejeune's test became public in two court cases,[10] the Court in subsequent decisions did not attempt to remove the arbitrariness in *Roe*'s definition of "person". As will be seen, this has led to a great deal of harm to both unborn children and the culture, tantamount to the harm caused in the *Dred Scott v. Sanford* decision 116 years before.

---

[10] See *Davis v. Davis*, 842 S.W. 2d 588, 597 (Tenn. Sup. Ct. 1992) and *New Jersey v. Alexander Loce* (N.J. Sup. Ct. 1991).

II.

PRINCIPLES OF ETHICS

Ethics is concerned with the good life, that is, the pursuit of what is good and the avoidance of what is evil or harmful. It is a much older pursuit than the study of reason and natural rights, because it seems to have been integral to human consciousness at its origin. It also appears to be connected with an equally originative human awareness of the sacred, transcendent, spiritual, and divine.[1] The human awareness of the sacred contains within itself an attraction toward the good and a revulsion for evil. These feelings of attraction and revulsion eventually become articulated into commandments for personal conduct and then become formulated into norms for a society and then codified as laws for a kingdom.

As philosophers, theologians, legal theorists, and political theorists reflected on the ground and legitimacy of law and the legal system, they noticed one particular ethical ground that seems to be universally present in every culture and religion, a ground without which all law and legal systems lose their intelligibility and legitimacy—namely, the principle of nonmaleficence (avoiding unnecessary harm to others, Principle 4). As we shall see, this great principle not only stands at the foundation of ethics and law, but also at

[1] See Mircea Eliade, ed., *The Encyclopedia of Religion*, 16 vols. (New York: Collier Macmillan, 1987).

the foundation of justice and rights. If this principle falls within a culture, then it is inevitable that the rest of ethics, justice, rights, and law will fall along with it. Therefore, it is deserving of the greatest respect and the greatest protection, for we cannot live long without it.

There are two important corollaries of the principle of nonmaleficence that are also vital to the intelligibility and grounding of law and rights: the principle of consistency of ends and means (Principle 5) and the principle of full human potential (Principle 6). This correlation will become evident in the explication below. For the moment, suffice it to say that without these three ethical principles, we may as well not proceed to the principles of justice and natural rights, for they would be unintelligible and without foundation.

Principle 4: The Principle of Nonmaleficence

Avoid unnecessary harms; if a harm is unavoidable, minimize it.

Silver Rule: Do *not* do unto others what you would *not* have them do unto you.

The principle of nonmaleficence dates back over three thousand years. It can be found in virtually every nation and in all the world's major religions. It is considered to be the most fundamental of all ethical principles, because if it falls, then all other ethical principles fall as well. Thus, it is the foundation for all ethics (and is sometimes called "ethical minimalism"). The principle may be stated as follows: "Do *not* do unto others what you would *not* have them do unto you." This might be translated as: "Do no unnecessary harm to another, but if a harm is unavoidable, do everything possible to minimize it."

Notice that this is like the Golden Rule (the principle of beneficence), with one important exception: the Silver Rule is focused on *avoiding harm* while the Golden Rule is focused on *doing good* ("Do unto others as you would have them do unto you"). This is why the Silver Rule is considered to be ethical minimalism while the Golden Rule (altruism, doing optimal good for others) is considered to be ethical maximalism.

Many thinkers consider the principle of nonmaleficence to be as fundamental to ethics as the principle of noncontradiction is to the rules of evidence. Why? Because its denial (1) entails the most fundamental form of injustice and (2) leads to an untenable social condition.

Let us examine the first rationale. It can be fairly said that no normal person (that is, someone who is not psychopathically masochistic) would like unnecessary harm done to himself. However, if one is not willing to fulfill this obligation toward others, one will commit the most fundamental form of injustice, namely, asking for something which one is not willing to extend to another. Justice, which is the condition necessary for a humane community and society, is, according to Plato, grounded in giving each person what he is owed.[2] Now, if others are obliged not to harm us unnecessarily, then we are obliged not to harm them unnecessarily. We cannot demand for ourselves what we are not willing to extend to others.

Secondly, failure to observe the principle of nonmaleficence is untenable. The moment we condone harming others unnecessarily, the fabric of community and society would unravel in theft, injury, violence, and even murder. Furthermore, interpersonal relationships would be impossible if we did not owe this duty to one another. Normally, we avoid

---

[2] See Plato, *Republic of Plato*, trans. Benjamin Jowett (New York: World Publishing, 1946), bk. 1, 331e.

people who say, "I really need to cause unnecessary harm to others in order to be fulfilled in my life", because we are likely to be the victims of that harm. Now if everyone is avoiding everybody else, there would be no relationship, community, or society.

The principle of nonmaleficence comes up very frequently in the life issues. For example, the *Roe v. Wade* decision violates the principle of nonmaleficence, because it justifies doing harm to a human being. As was established in Principle 3, a single-celled human zygote has a full human genome, and a developing human embryo has a highly actualized full human genome. Therefore, prima facie, the being in question is a human being, and allowing this human being to be killed under the law (whether in the first, second, or third trimester of pregnancy) is a particularly serious violation of the principle of nonmaleficence.

The "reasoning" of the majority of the Court in *Roe v. Wade* was grounded in a gratuitous and destructive assumption: when in doubt, *assume* that human life does not exist, and *assume*, as a consequence, that the killing of such life can be sanctioned. Attend to the majority's reasoning here:

> Texas urges that, apart from the Fourteenth Amendment, life begins at conception and is present throughout pregnancy, and that, therefore, the State has a compelling interest in protecting that life from and after conception. We need not resolve the difficult question of when life begins. When those trained in the respective disciplines of medicine, philosophy, and theology are unable to arrive at any consensus, the judiciary, at this point in the development of man's knowledge, is not in a position to speculate as to the answer.[3]

[3] *Roe v. Wade*, 410 U.S. 113 (1973), Sec. IX.B.

The obvious problem here is the majority's willingness to sanction killing through abortion when it was (by its own admission) *uncertain* about the presence of human life. If the judiciary did not believe that it was in a position to determine when human life begins, it should never have touched a case (let alone issued a decision) in which it might claim (let alone would claim) that human life was *not* present, which, if this claim is mistaken, would therefore sanction that life being killed. The principle of nonmaleficence requires that if one is not certain about the presence of human life, one must refrain from actions that could end a human life in the event that one is present. If one is uncertain about whether a being of human origin is really human, then one should presume that it is human because it came from human beings. To do otherwise is not only irresponsible (because one could illegitimately sanction killing out of uncertainty), but also unreasonable (because one should not expect anything other than human life to come from the reproduction of human beings).

The majority claimed that it consulted with many scientific, philosophical, and theological authorities, yet concluded in the absence of a consensus that the killing of human life is legally permissible. It never left open the possibility that new future technologies would be able more precisely to determine whether human life was present. Instead of deferring a decision about the case until such new technologies could resolve the question more clearly, it rushed toward a decision that amounts to a violation of the principle of nonmaleficence.

As mentioned above, a DNA sequencer was constructed in the late 1980s, which enabled Dr. Jerome Lejeune and others to be certain of the presence of a unique full human genome in a single-celled human zygote. As also noted above, a full human genome in a zygote (the initial cell formed when a *new* organism is produced by sexual reproduction) constitutes a distinct and unique human being whose identity and DNA is not reducible to the mother's. Dr. Lejeune later testified to this fact in 1991 in *New Jersey v. Alexander Loce* and in 1992 in *Davis v. Davis* (see note 10 on p. 19). This showed that the Supreme Court was unjustified in rushing toward its decision, which resulted in a violation of the principle of nonmaleficence, and that, if it were truly uncertain about whether a human being was present in the womb, it should have deferred any decision about abortion until new technologies could make a clear scientific determination about the presence of human life. The Court did not revisit the criteria used in the *Roe v. Wade* decision, which makes it at least as unjust as the *Dred Scott* decision. Recall that a majority's justification by uncertainty has a fundamental flaw, because uncertainty proves nothing objectively. It only manifests subjective ignorance. It is not the presence of evidence; it is the absence of the knowledge of evidence.

The majority enshrined this "irrational rationale" in a Supreme Court precedent. The highest court in the land declared that in the case of pregnancy when there is doubt about the presence of human life, it is justifiable to abort the fetus even though one may be killing a human being. One can see how this could be utilized very neatly to marginalize or harm, on the basis of uncertainty about personhood, people with physical defects, people who are becoming dependent on others (not completely autonomous), people who are less educated, and people from countries with an overall lesser degree of education. This absence of certainty has been used throughout history to attempt to justify bias, marginalization, segregation, oppression, and even genocide. Even the greatest skeptic about "slippery slope" arguments should feel some trepidation about doing this.

Persons—In Reality, Ethics, and the Law

As can be seen from the above, the majority's attempted justification of its actions turns on its definition of "person". Let us examine its "reasoning" here:

> If this suggestion of personhood is established, the appellant's case, of course, collapses, for the fetus' right to life would then be guaranteed specifically by the Amendment. The appellant conceded as much on reargument. On the other hand, the appellee conceded on reargument that no case could be cited that holds that a fetus is a person within the meaning of the Fourteenth Amendment. (Section IX.A)

The majority (and even the appellant seeking legal abortion), by their own admission, realized that if personhood could be established, then the appellant's case in favor of abortion would collapse. As will be shown below (Principle 7), this reasoning is backward. The Court did not have to *establish* the existence of personhood in a being of human origin with a full human genome. It should have *presumed* personhood in order to prevent a gross violation of the principle of nonmaleficence. This principle requires that the Court *establish* that personhood does *not* exist if it wants to sanction the killing of beings of human origin with a full human genome.

So what criterion did the majority use to try to establish the presence of personhood, when it did not use the criterion of "a being of human origin with a full human genome"? Remarkably, it searched for a previous *case* that acknowledged that a fetus was a person, and when it could not find one, it *assumed* that fetuses were not persons. This criterion is not sufficient to sanction a violation of the principle of nonmaleficence, because "personhood" is not merely a *legal* concept; it is essentially an *ontological* concept (i.e., it defines what a being is, namely, human) and an *ethical* concept (i.e., it defines the kind of being that we are obligated not to kill, abuse, or harm unnecessarily because of its intrinsic worth as human). The majority's claim that the absence of a *case* is sufficient to establish the nonpresence of personhood in a fetus, therefore, is a gigantic error of omission (Principle 1). It hasn't even begun to establish the nonpresence of personhood on either an ontological or an ethical level.

Let us now take a closer look at the notion of personhood, in order to address the error of the contention that the absence of a case precedent defining a human fetus to be a person is sufficient to establish the nonpresence of personhood in human fetuses. The term "person" was introduced into the English language prior to 1200 and was probably derived from the old French *persone/persoune*, which meant "human being". *Persone*, in turn, was probably derived from the Latin *persona*, which meant "human being, individual".[4] It is interesting to note that virtually every English dictionary today retains "human being" as the primary definition of "person". There is no linguistic evidence for contending that any being of human origin should *not* be considered to be a person; so the majority's decision to separate "human being" from "person" is highly unusual, if not unique. Such breaks from clear linguistic precedent frequently indicate spurious distinctions to justify problematic assertions. The majority's reasoning is a clear example of this problem.

The linguistic evidence shows that throughout its history, the word "person" has had a primarily ontological meaning, which defines words according to the nature of things, that is, what a thing is. Thus, "person" was inseparable from "a living individual human being". If the majority had made recourse to the linguistic history of "person" (and had, thereby, become acquainted with the ontological meaning of "person", a human being) before seeking a legal definition of it from case precedents, it would not have separated "person" from "human being" and would have presumed that the human fetus is a person because human fetuses are genetically distinct human organisms, rather than parts of human organisms. If the Court had waited for ten years, it would have found sufficient technological verification of this presumption through the DNA sequencer. Therefore, the majority would have had to have concluded on the basis of (1) linguistic usage and history, (2) common sense (human fetuses come from human beings), and (3) scientific evidence (the presence of a full human genome in a zygote; see above), that the human fetus is indisputably a person.

Instead of making recourse to the ontological definition of "person", the majority decided to restrict itself to a legal definition. It then found itself (conveniently) in need of a case precedent to determine whether a human fetus was a person. When (not surprisingly) it could not find such a case precedent (because the personhood of human fetuses had not previously been taken up by the United States Supreme Court), they concluded that human fetuses were not persons!

It is noteworthy that the well-known *Blackstone Commentaries on the Laws of England* and several *state* supreme courts did acknowledge the personhood of human fetuses and presumed that the killing of fetuses (as in abortion) was illegal, that allowing a fetus to die by neglecting medical treatment was actionable, and that negligence that caused harm to a fetus was also actionable.[5]

[5] The Supreme Court of Nevada ruled that a human fetus was a person for purposes of remedying personal fetal injuries allowing the child to sue after birth (see *Weaks v. Mounter*, 88 Nev. 118, 493 P. 2d 1307, 1309 [Nev. Sup. Ct. 1972]). The district court of the District of Columbia decided in 1971 that "a viable unborn child, which would have been born alive but for

In *Roe v. Wade*, the majority ignored these precedents and chose, rather, to argue a logical fallacy. This fallacy can be easily seen when one considers that every new definition of a term will never be found in a case precedent (old definitions) precisely because it is new. Trying to determine whether a human fetus is a person by means of U.S. Supreme Court case precedents when such cases had not previously arisen is like trying to establish the nonexistence of the North American continent prior to the time of Christopher Columbus by looking at maps made prior to his voyage, noticing the absence of any such continent, and concluding from its absence on these maps that it did not exist at that time. It is also like Einstein trying to validate his new theory of relativity based on the previous era's Newtonian assumptions. Einstein would have had to conclude that his theory was wrong because it is not to be found anywhere in Newtonian mechanics. Thankfully, the scientific world did not have to suffer from this self-contradictory methodology.

Inasmuch as the majority failed to look at the linguistic history of "person", failed to see the primary meaning of personhood as ontological (as a human being), failed to

---

the negligence of defendant, is a 'person' within meaning of Wrongful Death Statute" (see *Simmons v. Howard University*, 323 F. Supp. 529 [District of Columbia D.C. 1971], in *Black's Law Dictionary*, 5th ed. [St. Paul: West Publishing, 1979], p. 1029). In 1964, the Supreme Court of New Jersey ordered a pregnant woman who was a Jehovah's Witness to undergo a blood transfusion to save her life and that of her fetus (*Raleigh Fitkin-Paul Morgan Memorial Hospital v. Anderson* [N.J. Sup. Ct. 1964]). The courts of Georgia also held for the personhood of a fetus in 1951 when they allowed an action on behalf of a child who suffered a prenatal, but not fatal, injury at the hands of a negligent party carrying his mother to a hospital (*Tucker v. Howard Carmichael & Sons*, 208 Ga. 201, 65 Se. 2d 909 [Ga. Sup. Ct. 1951]). The courts explicitly declared that the fetus had rights independent of his mother and made frequent recourse to the *Blackstone Commentaries on the Laws of England*, which is quoted immediately below in this book.

assume that human parents would conceive human beings, failed to await potential scientific confirmation of the humanity of the fetus, and failed to correct itself when indisputable scientific confirmation of a full human genome in a single-celled human zygote became known, could it have done anything on the *legal* front to avert its highly problematic declaration on personhood? They could have done as the court of Georgia did in *Tucker v. Howard Carmichael & Sons*, when it cited the *Blackstone Commentaries on the Laws of England*. Note that the *Blackstone Commentaries* makes recourse precisely to a common usage and ontological definition:

> An infant *in ventre sa mere*, or in the mother's womb, is supposed in law to be born for many purposes. It is capable of having a legacy, or a surrender of a copyhold estate, made to it. It may have a guardian assigned to it; and it is enabled to have an estate limited to its use, and to take afterwards by such limitation, as if it were then actually born.[6]

If the majority had followed the example of the *Blackstone Commentaries*, the Georgia court in *Tucker v. Howard Carmichael & Sons*, the New Jersey Supreme Court in *Raleigh Fitkin-Paul Morgan Memorial Hospital v. Anderson*, the District of Columbia district court in *Simmons v. Howard University*, and the Nevada Supreme Court in *Weaks v. Mounter*[7] in turning to a common and ontological definition of personhood (instead of irrationally trying to find a legal definition from case precedents that had not yet considered the question), it would have come up with a very

---

[6] William Blackstone, *Commentaries on the Law: From the Abridged Edition of Wm. Hardcastle Browne* (Washington, D.C.: Washington Law Book, 1941), bk. 1, p. 130.

[7] All of these cases are cited in note 5 above.

different definition of personhood—one that did not break with either the common law or state supreme court precedent; one which did not introduce a spurious distinction between ontological personhood and legal personhood (based on a spurious distinction between "person" and "human being"); one that did not rush into an egregious violation of the principle of nonmaleficence through the arbitrary use of that spurious distinction; one that was legally and ethically responsible. The majority would have decided that "persons" are human beings, and that human fetuses are persons because they are human beings, which can be known by the fact that they are beings of human origin and can now be seen to have a full human genome irreducible to either one of his parents. It would have concluded in *Roe v. Wade* that the appellant's case collapsed, using its own reasoning that "if this suggestion of personhood is established, the appellant's case, of course, collapses, for the fetus' right to life would then be guaranteed specifically by the Amendment."

Can "person" be defined objectively? Recall from Principle 3 that adding criteria beyond the one objective criterion of "a being of human origin with a full human genome" is arbitrary. Thus, for example, we should not add "*fully actualized*" to the one objective criterion "being of human origin with a full human genome", because that addition is quite arbitrary (subjective). Does "fully actualized" mean a third-trimester fetus? A one-year-old infant? A ten-year-old child? An accomplished adult? As the age of "fully actualized" increases, do all of the less-actualized human beings suddenly cease to be "persons"?

We see not only problems with these additional criteria in the area of objectivity, but we also see it with respect to the principle of nonmaleficence. For example, if one tries to add a criterion such as "fully actualized" to the criterion of "a being of human origin with a full human genome", one would not only leave open the door for infanticide, but also the possibility of killing adolescents and even young adults (who may not have achieved full actualization). Inasmuch as one opens the door to additional harm by adding an arbitrary (subjective) criterion to the one objective criterion, then the addition of this arbitrary criterion violates the principle of nonmaleficence.

From the above, it can be seen that any proper consideration of personhood must begin with an objective criterion for a human being (namely, "a being of human origin with a full human genome"). This *objective* criterion for a human being is precisely what is meant by "ontological personhood", which must be the starting point for any proper consideration of ethical and legal personhood. Once it is established that a particular being is a human being, then it is established that the being has ontological personhood. Once ontological personhood is established, then ethical personhood follows. Ethical personhood simply means applying the principle of nonmaleficence (the most fundamental standard of ethics) to an ontological person (that is, to a human being). When we recognize the ethical personhood of a human being, we must recognize its legal personhood, because the law cannot undermine its most fundamental ethical standard (the principle of nonmaleficence) without undermining itself.

The immensely troubling dimension of the majority's rationale in *Roe v. Wade* is that it has now set within U.S. Supreme Court precedent its spurious distinction between ontological and legal personhood and sanctioned its irrational attempt to justify the nonpresence of personhood on the basis of case precedents that had not considered the question.

Legal personhood is not defined into existence by lawyers; it exists in the intrinsic worth of existing human beings.

When one separates legal personhood from ontological personhood, abuses always follow because one has to be a certain kind of human life in order to qualify for protection under the law. But every qualification is a form of exclusion and marginalization of some minority, which is an unnecessary harm. History is replete with examples of how this was done to Indians, black people, Jews, Gypsies, and all the victims of euthanasia (based on diminished capacity). It has now been done again using the same logic in the *Roe v. Wade* decision.

The above long string of logical errors leading to the sanctioning of a gross violation of the principle of nonmaleficence must give us pause. Could intelligent people really have done this without some degree of awareness of (and culpability for) its problematic character? Didn't they even have a hunch that something might be seriously wrong? The only way of redressing this wrong is to overturn the decision upon which it is based. This alone will restore the principle of nonmaleficence in our culture.

The Intrinsic Value of Persons

At this point, you may have surmised that the uncompromisable nature of the principle of nonmaleficence is grounded in the presumption that human beings have very special inherent or intrinsic value—and in the minds of many philosophers, *transcendent* value. Thus, human beings cannot be treated like mere inanimate objects or even like nonhuman animals. There is something about human beings that merits uncompromisable special protection, which does not allow for exceptions.

Some materialists might suggest that this specialness is completely unwarranted because, in their opinion, human beings are nothing more than a collection of material parts, and those material parts, in turn, are composed of other atomic and subatomic material parts. So why treat humans any better than any other material entity? Why can't we treat human beings like rocks, plants, or bugs? As will be explained below, most of us (from the most to the least technically trained) have had an awareness of being more than the sum of our material parts. This awareness is not restricted to religiously or spiritually inclined people, nor to philosophers such as Plato and Aristotle; it pervades the common sense of virtually every human being.

Before delving into a more technical explanation of the above, we should remember that it is no different to say that "persons have intrinsic value" as to say that "human beings have intrinsic value". It is necessary to do so in order to (1) ground the definition of personhood in objective evidence (Principle 3) and (2) prevent serious violations of the principle of nonmaleficence (Principle 4). Thus, if human beings have intrinsic (and even transcendent) value, so also do persons.

So why do philosophers, scientists, and people of common sense assert that human beings have such a special value? The answer lies in several interrelated observations, which will be discussed below. These observations are present in the works of many philosophers and scientists,[8] beginning with Socrates, Plato, and Aristotle, moving through Saint Augustine, Maimonides, Averroes, Saint Thomas Aquinas, Francisco Suarez, John Locke, Immanuel Kant, G. W. F. Hegel, John Henry Newman, and into the twentieth and twenty-first centuries (e.g., Edmund Husserl, Edith Stein, Jacques Maritain, Henri Bergson, Emerich Coreth, Bernard

---

[8] The origin of this idea precedes the advent of formal philosophy and science and can be found in a large number of religions that are premised on the spiritual powers of human beings. Judaism formalized this belief (see Genesis 1–2), which was transmitted to Christianity, and later to Islam.

Lonergan, and many others). This idea is also central to the works of many prominent physicists and biologists in the twentieth and twenty-first centuries. Two examples of this will suffice to make our point. The first comes from the great physicist Sir Arthur Eddington, who observed, after detailing the equations of quantum physics and relativity physics:

> We all know that there are regions of the human spirit untrammelled by the world of physics. In the mystic sense of the creation around us, in the expression of art, in a yearning towards God, the soul grows upward and finds the fulfillment of something implanted in its nature. The sanction for this development is within us, a striving born within our consciousness or an Inner Light proceeding from a greater power than ours. Science can scarcely question this sanction, for the pursuit of science springs from a striving which the mind is impelled to follow, a questioning that will not be suppressed. Whether in the intellectual pursuits of science or in the mystical pursuits of the spirit, the light beckons ahead and the purpose surging in our nature responds.[9]

The eminent geneticist Francis Collins, director of the Human Genome Project, expresses a similar insight:

> As the director of the Human Genome Project, I have led a consortium of scientists to read out the 3.1 billion letters of the human genome, our own DNA instruction book. As a believer, I see DNA, the information molecule of all living things, as God's language, and the elegance and complexity of our own bodies and the rest of nature as a reflection of God's plan.... Can you both pursue an

[9] Arthur Eddington, *The Nature of the Physical World* (Cambridge: Cambridge University Press, 1928), pp. 327–28.

understanding of how life works using the tools of genetics and molecular biology, and worship a creator God? Aren't
evolution and faith in God incompatible? Can a scientist
believe in miracles like the resurrection? Actually, I find
no conflict here, and neither apparently do the 40 percent
of working scientists who claim to be believers.[10] ... I
have found there is a wonderful harmony in the comple-
mentary truths of science and faith. The God of the Bible
is also the God of the genome. God can be found in the
cathedral or in the laboratory. By investigating God's majestic and awesome creation, science can actually be a means
of worship.[11]

If the human genome can be viewed as the language of
God, then human beings can be viewed as the consummate
expression of that language, and it is not unwarranted to
say, from a scientific and faith perspective, that human beings
are made in the image of God. As expressed in the Book of
Genesis, "So God created man in his own image, in the
image of God he created him; male and female he created
them" (1:27; RSV, 2nd ed.).

So what is the philosophical and scientific origin of this
belief in the specialness (and transcendence) of human beings?
It is predominantly grounded in a longstanding observation
about nonhuman animals, which continues to be verified
in recent empirical investigations. Bernard Lonergan expresses
it as follows:

[I]t is only when [animals'] functioning is disturbed that they
enter into consciousness. Indeed, not only is a large part of

---

[10] More than 40% of scientists are believers. Many prefer not to profess
their faith in a public scientific setting.

[11] Francis Collins, "Collins: Why This Scientist Believes in God", *CNN.com*,
April 3, 2007, http://www.cnn.com/2007/US/04/03/collins.commentary/
index.html.2007.

animal living nonconscious, but the conscious part itself is intermittent. Animals sleep. It is as though the full-time business of living called forth consciousness as a part-time employee, occasionally to meet problems of malfunctioning, but regularly to deal rapidly, effectively, and economically with the external situations in which sustenance is to be won and into which offspring are to be born. . . . When the object fails to stimulate, the subject is indifferent; and when nonconscious vital process has no need of outer objects, the subject dozes and falls asleep.[12]

This might be summarized quite simply as follows. When animals run out of biological opportunities and dangers, they fall asleep. When you stop feeding your dog, or giving it affection and attention (biological opportunities), and introduce no biological dangers (such as a predator) into its sensorial purview, it will invariably and inevitably fall asleep.

In stark contrast to this, when human beings run out of biological opportunities and dangers, they frequently ask questions, seek purpose or meaning in life, contemplate beauty, think about the goodness (or imperfections) of their beloveds, think about unfairness or injustice and how to make their situation or the world better, and even think about mathematics, physics, philosophy, and theology—for their own sake.[13] When human beings run out of biological opportunities and dangers, they generally do not fall asleep; they engage in what Plato and his followers (the

[12] Bernard Lonergan, *The Lonergan Reader*, ed. Mark Morelli and Elizabeth Morelli (Toronto: University of Toronto Press, 1997), pp. 108–9.

[13] "When an animal has nothing to do it goes to sleep. When a man has nothing to do he may ask questions. The first moment is an awakening to one's intelligence. It is release from the dominance of biological drive and from the routines of everyday living. It is the effective emergence of wonder, of the desire to understand" (ibid., p. 54).

Neoplatonists) called "transcendental activities". These activities reveal the specialness of human beings, which makes them deserving of special consideration.

The Neoplatonists identified five areas of transcendental activity (termed "the five transcendentals"): the awareness of and desire for Truth, Love, Goodness, Beauty, and Being. They are called "transcendental" because they all seem to have a limitless horizon, and human beings seem to be aware of their limitless possibilities and seem to desire their perfect (limitless) fulfillment. Thus, in the view of many philosophers, mathematicians, and scientists, human beings seem to have an awareness of and desire for *perfect and unconditional* Truth, Love, Goodness, Beauty, and Being. (A more detailed explanation of these five transcendental desires is given in the appendix of this book.)

Since these five transcendentals are necessarily beyond all algorithmically finite structures (which determine all *physical* realities and laws constituting subatomic particles, molecules, cells, and complex organic structures such as a brain), many philosophers, mathematicians, and scientists have held that human beings are more than mere matter. Human beings seem to have a transmaterial or spiritual power or dimension that enables them to move beyond every algorithmically finite structure (physical structure) and to be creative in ways that defy the possibilities of artificial intelligence.

Interestingly, this claim is corroborated in the domain of mathematics by Kurt Gödel (in the famous theorem named after him). He anticipated the limits of artificial intelligence that are defied by human intelligence on a regular basis. Essentially, Gödel showed that there will always be unprovable propositions within any set of axiomatic statements in mathematics. Human beings are able not only to show that consistent, unprovable statements exist, but also to prove that they are consistent by making recourse to axioms *beyond* those used to generate these statements. Artificial intelligence is incapable of doing this. This reveals that human thinking is not based on a set of prescribed axioms, rules, or programs, and is, by nature, *beyond* such prescribed rules and programs.[14]

As noted in the appendix of this book, the evidence of the transmaterial (spiritual) dimension of human beings is quite significant. If one is to deny this transmaterial dimension, one will simply have to ignore the stark differences between animal and human consciousness; to ignore human awareness of the limitless horizons of Truth, Love, Goodness, Beauty, and Being; to ignore the remarkable properties of human creativity explicated by Gödel; and to ignore the natural human capacity to seek a transcendent God. If one feels uncertain about writing off this body of evidence, then it is unjustifiable to rush into materialistic reductionism, naïve identifications of animal and human intelligence, and a denial of the human capacity for self-transcendence. But if one stops short of these simplistic positions, one remains open to the specialness of human beings, and therefore open to their special value. The principle of nonmaleficence requires that if we are uncertain about whether transmaterial and self-transcendent qualities exist in human beings, we must presume that these qualities are present, for failure to do so will entail a serious violation of the foundation of all ethics and law.

---

[14] The theorem was published by Kurt Gödel ("Über formal unentscheidbare Sätze der Principia Mathematica und verwandter Systeme I", *Monatshefte für Mathematik und Physik* 38 [1931]: 173–98) and was revised by John R. Lucas ("Minds, Machines, and Gödel", *Philosophy* 36 [1961]: 120), and by the eminent physicist Roger Penrose (*The Emperor's New Mind* [Oxford: Oxford University Press, 1989]). An excellent summary of Lucas' rendition of Gödel's proof may be found in Stephen M. Barr, *Modern Physics and Ancient Faith* (Notre Dame: University of Notre Dame Press, 2003), p. 214.

Principle 5: The Principle of Consistent Ends and Means

The end does not justify the means.

This great ethical dictum has roots in classical philosophy, but was formalized in its current form in Augustine's work *Contra Mendacium* (*Against Lying*; see vii). The concept is applied to the whole of ethics by Aquinas in his *Summa Theologica* (I–II, q. 20, a. 2). It may be summarized as follows: "One cannot use an evil means to achieve a good end; the evil of the means will undermine the goodness of the end." It may alternatively be phrased: "One cannot use an unjust means to attain a just end; the injustice of the means will undermine the justice of the end."

There is one seeming exception to this rule which enjoys agreement among many ethical theorists, namely, that one can use an *objectively* wrong means (such as lying) to *prevent* a greater evil (such as murder). Preventing "a greater evil" is taken to be a good end one may obtain by using an objectively wrong means, provided the evil of the means is less than the evil of the end to be prevented. An "objectively wrong act" refers to an *act* being unjust in itself or evil in itself. This is recognized in the law by the phrase *malum in se*, "evil by its very nature", and is distinguished from *malum prohibitum*, "wrong because it is proscribed by law". It is used here to distinguish an objectively wrong *act* from a *person's* subjective culpability.

Thus, on the view outlined above, a person can commit an *objectively* wrong act without being *subjectively* culpable (or blamable) when that action prevents or circumvents an objectively greater evil.

This apparent exception to the principle of consistent means and ends, which is frequently termed "the lesser of two evils", has been famously used to justify self-defense and just wars. Many ethical theorists do not accept the principle; some reject the idea that circumstances ever justify committing an objectively wrong act. Others go further and claim that there are no objective criteria by which "evils" can be adequately compared in order to determine the "lesser evil" that may be committed to prevent the "greater evil".

What's more, many ethicists distinguish *"committing an act* that is supposedly the lesser of two evils, in order to prevent the greater evil", from *"tolerating a lesser evil* because one cannot act to eliminate the evil without creating a greater evil". The latter may never be done, while the former may. In this view, one does not *do* evil by *tolerating* an evil that one *cannot* eliminate without making a situation worse.

Notwithstanding the above points, let us assume, for the sake of argument, that in at least some cases the principle of committing the "lesser of two evils" to prevent the "greater evil" is ethically legitimate. We can restate the principle as follows: "One may not use an objectively wrong or unjust means to attain a good or just end if that end does not prevent a greater evil than the wrong or unjust means one employs to achieve it."

Thus, a group of people cannot take out an insurance policy on another person and then bring that person to an early demise (even with a last excellent meal) so that the insurance proceeds can be collected to give to charities, like their school or hospital or church. Even though giving money to charity is a good end, it does not justify the objectively wrong means of killing the person, because the group is not preventing any greater objective evil by killing her.

This principle comes into play frequently in the life issues. It has been argued that in order to achieve the good end of allowing a woman to have custody over her own body, the law should allow the killing of unborn human beings. This is a clear case of using an objectively wrong means to attain a good end. Does the exception of the "lesser of two evils" apply here, assuming, for the sake of argument, that the exception is legitimate? When one ranks the objective wrongs in question (the killing of an unborn human being versus disallowing a woman custody over her own body), it is commonly acknowledged that killing is a greater injustice than disallowing custody over one's body, because killing life is more serious than restricting an aspect of life.[15]

Now, some have argued that the killing of a human being here is justified because the human being is unborn; that is, either the dependence of the human being on his mother or the incomplete actualization of his development mitigates the objective wrong of the act of killing. But the fallaciousness of this "reasoning" can be seen prima facie and through Principle 3 (the principle of objective evidence) and Principle 4 (the principle of nonmaleficence).

Why is this reasoning fallacious prima facie? Because the dependency and state of actualization of a human being does not mitigate its humanness. As noted above, humanness is determined by the presence of a full and distinctive human genome in a human zygote. The "full and distinctive human genome in a human zygote" does not cease to be present because the human being is dependent on someone else or because he has not completed his development or there is impairment to his full development. Now, insofar as these factors do not mitigate the unborn human being's humanness, they do not mitigate the objective wrong of killing him.

Why does this "reasoning" violate Principle 3? Recall that Principle 3 requires objective (publicly verifiable) evidence, instead of merely arbitrary subjective preferences, and states that one cannot qualify an objective criterion with an

---

[15] This will come up again with respect to Principle 8, which concerns determining which rights are most fundamental in "rights conflicts".

additional arbitrary subjective criterion. When one uses a human being's dependency or state of development to qualify the objective principle of the presence of a human being (indicated by the presence of a full and distinct human genome in a human zygote) it makes the objective criterion into an arbitrary and subjective one. Who qualifies as dependent? An unborn human being? A one-year-old? A ten-year-old? A person with physical challenges? An elderly person? Is the humanity of these people questionable because of their dependence on others? The objectivity of the presence of a human being has been made arbitrary and subjective by adding an arbitrary and subjective qualifier.

We have also seen how the addition of these arbitrary and subjective criteria leads to violations of Principle 4, the principle of nonmaleficence. By qualifying the humanness of a being with a full human genome through the addition of "dependency on others" or "incompleteness of development", one "justifies" not only the possibility of killing the unborn, but also the one-year-old, the ten-year-old, the person with physical challenges, and the elderly person. Note that I did not say one opens the door to the *possibility* of "justifying" these killings, but rather that this reasoning *actually* "justifies" these killings, and so it actually "justifies" a serious violation of the principle of nonmaleficence. Again, even the greatest skeptic of the "slippery slope" argument should feel some trepidation here.

There is one other well-known qualifier to the dictum that the end does not justify the means, termed the "principle of double effect".[16] It states that in situations where one commits an act that is good or neutral in itself, but which

[16] The principle of double effect originates in the thought of Thomas Aquinas in his treatment of self-defense. See Aquinas, *Summa Theologica*, trans. Fathers of the English Dominican Province (New York: Benziger Brothers, 1948), II–II, q. 64, a. 7, vol. 2, pp. 1471–72.

has two effects, one good and one bad, and one intends only the good, then one is not morally culpable for the bad effect (if it should arise). It also states that in situations where one does X with the intention to achieve a morally justified end but which through no fault of the agent the end is not achieved and a bad result occurs, then one is not morally culpable for that bad effect. If one intends to save a life by means of surgery, which not only causes harm to the body, but also risks the possibility of worse injury or death, one is justified in taking the risk in order to save a life. If something goes wrong and the surgery causes greater injury or death, one cannot be held accountable for the death, because the intention of doing the surgery was to *save* a life.

This exception comes up frequently in the administration of pain protocols, such as morphine, during times of serious injury or terminal illness. If a physician's intention is to prevent pain, without *intending* death, and the administration of the morphine should cause the cessation of breathing, then the physician should not be held accountable for the death of a person whose pain he was simply trying to alleviate.

Principle 6: The Principle of Full Human Potential

Every human being (or group of human beings) deserves to be valued according to the full level of human development, not according to the level of development currently achieved.

This principle is a derivative of Principle 4. It may be stated as follows:

> In order to prevent a violation of the principle of nonmaleficence, every human being must be valued at his highest

potential level of development, because attaching value to any lower level of development risks the possibility of under-valuing that human being (i.e., subjecting him to the clas-sification of being "inferior" or "less than human"). This undervaluation, in turn, allows for a serious violation of the principle of nonmaleficence, that is, justifying killing, slavery, marginalization, isolation, etc., of this human being because the human being is thought to be "inferior" or "less than human".[17]

This principle originated with the Dominican friar Bar-tolomé de las Casas, who attempted to defend the Indians of the New World against the Spanish slave traders and the Span-ish court in the middle half of the sixteenth century. In a famous debate with Juan Ginés de Sepúlveda, las Casas (who held two degrees in canon law) made a valiant defense of the rights of the Indians against Sepúlveda, who claimed that because the Indians had not yet achieved an advanced cul-ture (like that of the Europeans), they could be judged to be inferior barbarians (less than human), which, in turn,

---

[17] It should be noted that this judgment or valuation of human beings is both a judgment in principle (i.e., a judgment according to inherent good-ness or justice) and a practical judgment (a judgment that must be rendered because failure to do so risks a radical violation of the principle of nonmaleficence).

An important distinction must be made at this juncture. There may be some human beings who will not be able to achieve the full capacity of human *nature* because of a deficiency in their initial condition or an imped-iment in the process of their development (which may affect their physical, mental, or psychological actualization). Should we judge these individuals according to the fullest potential of *human nature* or according to the fullest potential that these *individuals* will be likely to achieve? Though the Domin-ican friar Bartolomé de las Casas did not discuss this question, we may be able to infer an answer from his *principle*—namely, that we should accord all human beings a value or dignity according to the fullest capacity of *human nature* because this is the only way of assuring that we will not seriously violate the principle of nonmaleficence.

justified their enslavement by the Spanish conquerors. This justification extended to the killing of the Indians if they resisted the "just" enslavement by their conquerors. It should be noted here that this same rationale has been used in attempts to justify all forms of slavery and genocide throughout history.

Las Casas was not only horrified by the attempt of Sepúlveda to justify the killing of Indians who resisted "just" enslavement; he recognized that the attempt to give this justification legal sanction in the Spanish court would undermine the mores and culture of Spain and other enslaving nations. Not surprisingly, he disputed the first contention of Sepúlveda, namely, that the Indians were inferior people ("barbarians", less than human). He showed that although the Indians had not yet achieved the same degree of technological civilization and scientific knowledge of the Spanish, they showed the *potential* to achieve every bit as much if given the time and opportunity. Furthermore, most of the Indians displayed far more civilized moral conduct than the bloodthirsty conquerors who oppressed, injured, and killed them. From this, it could be reasoned that the Indians were every bit as human as the Spanish; they had simply not developed to the same degree in certain aspects of technological and scientific knowledge.

Las Casas extended this analysis to people of every region of the world through the following reasoning: "We find that for the most part men are intelligent, far sighted, diligent, and talented, so that it is impossible for a whole region or country to be slow witted and stupid, moronic, or suffering from similar natural defects or abnormalities."[18] Las Casas'

---

[18] Bartolomé de las Casas, *In Defense of the Indians: The Defense of the Most Reverend Lord, Don Fray Bartolomé de las Casas, of the Order of Preachers, Late Bishop of Chiapa, against the Persecutors and Slanderers of the Peoples of the New World Discovered across the Seas*, trans. and ed. Stafford Poole (DeKalb: Northern Illinois University Press, 1992), p. 38.

logic is clear. Since human beings have been found to be "intelligent, far sighted, diligent, and talented" in virtually every region of the world, we should presume that this is the case whenever a new group of people is discovered, even if that new group has not yet reached the state of technology or development attained by another group. It is our ethical obligation (in order to avoid a serious violation of the principle of nonmaleficence) to presume what can be fairly inferred from the vast majority of mankind: that all groups, and the vast majority of individuals, will reach a naturally high potential of intelligence, far-sightedness, diligence, and talent if given the time and opportunity.

With las Casas' foundation, we can see two important consequences for the maintenance and progress of humaneness and civility:

(1)   A people cannot be justifiably branded "less than human" because of their degree of development if they show the potential to achieve that development in the future. The potential to achieve a full level of development is sufficient to establish the nature of the being. Thus, the Indians' potential to achieve a full degree of human development is sufficient to establish their humanity. The fact that they had not yet reached their full development was not an indication of lesser nature, but only an indication of accidents or occasions which may have prevented or delayed that full development. It is erroneous to make a judgment about "nature" on the basis of mere accidents or historical occasion, for nature is indicated by the power or potential of something, not by the accidents or processes which occasion a particular achievement of that potential or power.

(2)   If a people is unjustifiably judged inferior (by erroneously judging accidents or historical occasions instead

of potential or power), then the harm which arises out of that erroneous judgment is a clear violation of the principle of nonmaleficence; and if that violation of the principle leads to the enslavement or death of an innocent human being, then the violators can justifiably be held responsible for the injustice.

The reader can probably see the parallel between las Casas' debate with Sepúlveda and the life issues which are being debated today. All we need to do is substitute the words "unborn human being" for the words "people" and "Indian" in the above two consequences of las Casas' reasoning. The italicized portions below indicate the substitutions.

(1)   An *unborn human being* cannot be justifiably branded "less than human" because of its degree of development if it shows the potential to achieve that development in the future. The potential to achieve full development is sufficient to establish the nature of the being. Thus, the *unborn human being's* potential to achieve a full degree of human development is sufficient[19] to establish his humanity. The fact that

[19] Note the difference between a "*sufficient* criterion" and a "*necessary* criterion". When a sufficient criterion is present then a particular fact is established, but if a sufficient criterion is *not* present it does *not negate* the reality of a fact. Thus, if an unborn human being has the potential for full human development, he or she must be considered a full human being. However, if that unborn human being does not have a potential for full human development, it does *not* negate the humanity of that unborn being. Such an inference is a logical fallacy called "negating the antecedent" (see below page 69). A necessary criterion is quite different, because it expresses a "*sine qua non*" ("a that without which"). This criterion shows what is *necessary* for something to be human because it refers to the most fundamental or essential defining characteristic of a given reality. For example, in the particular case under consideration, the essential defining characteristic of a human being would be either "the presence of a human genome" or "origin through human parents". If either one of these two essentially defining characteristics

he has not yet reached his full development is not an indication of a nature that is subhuman, but only an indication of accidents or occasions which may have prevented or delayed that full development. It is erroneous to make a judgment about "nature" on the basis of mere accidents or historical occasion, for nature is indicated by the power or potential of something, not by the accidents or processes which occasion a particular achievement of that potential or power.

(2) If an *unborn human being* is unjustifiably judged less than human (by erroneously judging accidents or historical occasions instead of potential or power), then the harm which arises out of that erroneous judgment is a clear violation of the principle of nonmaleficence; and if that violation of the principle leads to the enslavement or death of an innocent human being, then the violators can justifiably be held responsible for the injustice.

The consequence of denying las Casas' principle is so serious that one must be careful not to attempt justifying such a denial on the basis of sophistry; yet sophistry is precisely what is required to deny it because a denial requires that one assert that the nature of a being is determined by its stage of development rather than its natural capacity for full development.

Now let us examine how the majority in the *Roe v. Wade* decision used its own version of Sepúlveda's reasoning to attempt to justify judging the human fetus according to its stage of development (instead of its actualizable power or

---

is *not* present, then the reality in question is *not* a human being. There can be many sufficient criteria to establish the presence of human beings, but not all of them are necessary criteria.

potential). Notice that the majority arbitrarily divided fetal development into three stages (trimesters) declaring that states could take greater interest to prevent the killing of a fetus in only the last stage, which implied that greater degrees of personhood were attached to the later stages of fetal development than earlier ones:

> (a) For the stage prior to approximately the end of the first trimester, the abortion decision and its effectuation must be left to the medical judgment of the pregnant woman's attending physician [and the state has virtually no power to regulate it].
> (b) For the stage subsequent to approximately the end of the second trimester, the State, in promoting its interest in the health of the mother, may, if it chooses, regulate the abortion procedure in ways that are reasonably related to maternal health.
> (c) For the stage subsequent to viability, the State, in promoting its interest in the potentiality of human life, may, if it chooses, regulate, and even proscribe, abortion except where necessary, in appropriate medical judgment, for the preservation of the life or health of the mother. (*Roe v. Wade*, 3A–3C)

The idea of "degrees of personhood" is quite troubling, because, as implied above, it can be used in attempting to justify every form of bias, prejudice, marginalization, and even imprisonment and death on the basis of a completely *arbitrary* criterion. This is precisely what justice and law were meant to prevent. How can the highest court in the land legitimize a train of thought which undermines the principle of justice which it is sworn to uphold? Again, the only way of extricating ourselves from this grossly unethical error is to overturn the decision and thinking process that attempted to justify it.

III.

PRINCIPLES OF JUSTICE AND NATURAL RIGHTS

The principle of natural rights (Principle 7) is an extension of the principle of nonmaleficence, for *any* denial or negation of these rights will always entail a serious violation(s) of the principle of nonmaleficence. Inasmuch as these two principles go hand in hand, the principle of natural rights is as necessary as the principle of nonmaleficence in grounding the intelligibility and the legitimacy of all laws and legal systems.

There are two important corollaries of the principle of natural rights that are also vital to the intelligibility and legitimacy of all law and legal systems, namely, the principle of the fundamentality of rights (Principle 8) and the principle of limits to freedom (Principle 9). This correlation will be justified in the explication below. As with the principle of nonmaleficence, the principle of natural rights and its corollaries must be protected, for this principle differentiates just laws from unjust laws, and just legal systems from unjust legal systems. As will become clear, unjust laws must be resisted not only to protect those who would become their victims, but also to shore up the legal systems that will ultimately be undermined by their perpetuation.

Principle 7: The Principle of Natural Rights

All human beings possess in themselves (by virtue of their existence alone) the inalienable rights of life, liberty, and property ownership; no government gives these rights, and no government can take them away.

Justice is the foundation of law and civil order. It was originally defined by Plato as giving each person his due,[1] and is an application of the principle of nonmaleficence in the arena of society and state (because not giving people what they are owed causes unjustifiable and unnecessary harm). As will be explained below, the principle of justice reached both its bedrock and flourishing in the principle of natural rights, which originated with a seventeenth-century Spanish Jesuit, Francisco Suarez, in a 1610 tractate entitled *De Legibus* (*On the Laws*).[2] Since Suarez was the most widely read among the Scholastic philosophers of his day, it is reasonable to assume that John Locke and other legal theorists of Locke's time were familiar with Suarez's breakthrough discovery,[3] which probably helped Locke to formulate his well-known theory of natural rights in the *Second Treatise on Government*:

> Man being born, as has been proved, with a title to perfect freedom, and an uncontrolled enjoyment of all the rights

[1] See Plato, *Republic*, bk. 1, 331e.

[2] For the origin of our contemporary understanding of the natural rights theory, see John Finnis, *Natural Law and Natural Rights* (New York: Oxford University Press, 1980), pp. 206–7.

[3] This is borne out by the fact that Locke seems to borrow Suarez's understanding of rights as "claims". See J. Tully, *A Discourse on Property: John Locke and His Adversaries* (New York: Cambridge University Press, 1980), p. 67. Furthermore, Suarez influenced Grotius, who, in turn, influenced Hobbes, who, in turn, influenced Locke; so there is at least an indirect connection.

and privileges of the law of nature, equally with any other man, or number of men in the world, hath by nature a power, ... to preserve his property, that is, his life, liberty and estate, against the injuries and attempts of other men.[4]

Locke influenced Thomas Jefferson, who placed Locke's inalienable rights theory within the Declaration of Independence: "We hold these truths to be self-evident, that all men are created equal, that they are endowed by their Creator with certain unalienable Rights, that among these are Life, Liberty and the pursuit of Happiness." Before examining this text, it may be helpful to get a deeper insight into the history and meaning of rights.

Perhaps the best known medieval tractate on natural law was written by Saint Thomas Aquinas in 1270. Like Plato and Aristotle, he saw the natural ground of law in the principle of justice (*iustitia*), which seeks a right relationship among human beings. Suarez moved the ground of law from a right *relationship* (justice) to the right (*jus*) of *individuals*. He believes that the "true, strict and proper meaning [of *jus*] ... is a kind of moral power which every man has, either over his own property or with respect to that which is due to him."[5] This interpretation of *jus*, according to John Finnis, "crossed a watershed" into the idea of natural rights.[6]

Suarez believed that "a right was something that a man had as his own, that he could exercise in his own name, [and] that could not be taken away from him without

[4] John Locke, *Second Treatise on Government*, ed. C.B. Macpherson (Indianapolis: Hackett Publishing, 1980), p. 46.

[5] Francisco Suarez, *De Legibus* (Madrid: Consejo Superior de Investigaciones Científicas, Instituto Francisco de Vitoria, 1971), 1.2.5.

[6] See Finnis, *Natural Law and Natural Rights*, p. 207.

injustice." [7] This was highly significant, because it meant that a state or governing body does *not* confer natural rights on individuals, which would allow that state to take those rights away. Instead, Suarez noted, natural rights belong to human beings by their *very human existence*, and these inherent possessions cannot be taken away without injustice. Thus, a state cannot take away a human being's natural rights by means of a court order or by its constitution, by a vote of the majority, or even by a vote of a supermajority. The state (or the people constituting that state) cannot take away what does not belong to them without perpetrating an extreme injustice. [8]

Suarez did not arbitrarily assert this principle. He grounded it in two ways. First, like Locke and Jefferson after him, he appealed to divine authority, namely, that all human beings are endowed by the *Creator* with rights that are necessary for the preservation and perfection of their human nature. However, Suarez's second justification of inalienable rights (his more developed justification) is a natural one, because it does not appeal to endowment by a Creator. It is grounded in the nature of law itself. He holds that all prescriptive

---

[7] Brian Tierney, *The Idea of Natural Rights: Studies on Natural Rights, Natural Law, and Church Law, 1150–1625* (Atlanta: Scholars Press, 1997), pp. 307–8 (citing Suarez in *De statu perfectionis, Opera* 15.8.5.29, 571).

[8] Some readers may be wondering whether the state has the right to punish—would not incarceration be taking away a person's liberty rights? Though Suarez does not discuss the problem of rights and state punishment, John Locke does. In his *Second Treatise on Government*, he indicates that a state has the right to punish an individual who is violating the rights of others in order to protect both natural rights and natural law. When a person violates the rights of others he forsakes the rights that he possesses. He allows the state to limit or condition his own rights. Tuckness describes Locke's rationale as follows: "Since the fundamental law of nature is that mankind be preserved and since that law would 'be in vain' with no human power to enforce it, it must therefore be legitimate for individuals to punish each other even before government exists" (A. Tuckness, "Locke's Political Philosophy", *Stanford Encyclopedia of Philosophy Online*, Fall 2010 ed., http://plato.stanford.edu/entries/locke-political).

laws (made by monarchs, legislatures, or courts) have the same end and purpose, namely, "the due preservation and natural perfection or happiness of human nature".[9]

Suarez recognized not only the right to life (*preserving* human nature) and the right to liberty and happiness (*perfecting* human nature and happiness), but also that these three rights, which belong to a human being by his very existence, were the grounds upon which all other laws stood. If a state (i.e., the executive, legislative, or judicial authorities of that state) failed to protect these natural rights, then the prescriptive laws (i.e., statutes and court rulings) would lose their *intrinsic* end and purpose. All prescriptive laws would then become the mere extrinsic arbitrary assertions of governmental authorities. They would be arbitrary because they would be devoid of intrinsic purpose. This argument was particularly powerful at the time of Suarez because of the many abuses of state power which occurred because these states did not feel bound by the *intrinsic* purpose of law. The same holds true today. If a state (through its executive, legislative, or judicial branches) fails first and foremost to protect the natural rights of *all* human beings, then that state undermines the intrinsic purpose of the law and gives itself the power to act in an arbitrary way by sheer dint of its power.

Let us now return to the Declaration of Independence. Notable is that the passage concerning inalienable rights does not appear in the Bill of Rights in the Constitution. The Bill of Rights and the Constitution were understood by the Founding Fathers to be *extrinsic* declarations concerned with rights brought into existence by a people or a state. These extrinsic rights are quite distinct from natural rights or inalienable rights, which are not brought into existence by a state

---

[9] Suarez, *De Legibus*, 3.2.7.7, 118.

because they belong to all human beings by their very
existence. This can be seen by comparing the preambles of
the Constitution and the Declaration of Independence. The
opening words of the Constitution's Preamble are:

> We the *People* of the *United States*, in Order to form a more
> perfect *Union*, establish Justice, insure [sic] *domestic* Tran-
> quility, provide for the *common* defense, promote the *general*
> Welfare, and secure the Blessings of Liberty to *ourselves* and
> our Posterity, do ordain and establish this Constitution for
> the *United States of America*. (Italics mine.)

Notice that the Constitution is concerned with the *extrinsically declared* rights and obligations of the *group* ("*People
of the United States*", "*Union*", "*domestic* Tranquility", "*common* defense", "*general* Welfare", "*ourselves*"). In contrast to
this, the Declaration of Independence is concerned with
the natural or inalienable rights belonging to all human
beings in themselves. These inalienable rights are *recognized* to be *self-evident,* but not extrinsically authorized by
a people. This gives us a clue about why natural rights do
not appear in the Bill of Rights or the Constitution as a
whole. It is probable that the writers of the Constitution
recognized that *natural* rights did not require *extrinsic* authorization. They probably believed, as Jefferson did, that *natural* rights were *self*-evident, and there are no requirements
for additional justification or authorization.[10] Indeed, such

---

[10] Alexander Hamilton and other Federalists went so far as to say that if the
state attempted to define rights in a Bill of Rights, it might have the effect of
limiting rights to those listed in the U.S. Constitution (which could inadver-
tently allow the government to ignore or disallow *natural* rights that are not
listed in the Constitution), and so they favored leaving out the Bill of Rights
altogether (see Federalist no. 84, in Alexander Hamilton, John Jay, and James
Madison, *The Federalist Papers*, McLean edition, Library of Congress, etext
by Project Gutenberg, 1788, http://thomas.loc.gov/home/histdox/fed

extrinsic authorization would have been self-contradictory. They probably also recognized that self-evident natural rights were the ground and purpose of all legitimate governmental and legal authority, and therefore the ground and purpose of the Constitution itself. They probably also recognized that a failure to defend the natural rights of individuals would not only undermine the Constitution, but would also make their power quite arbitrary (which was precisely what they were attempting to avoid in their new government).

Thomas Paine explicitly held this view in his treatise on *The Rights of Man* (1791), where he declared: "The fact therefore must be that the individuals themselves, each in his own personal and sovereign right, entered into a contract with each other to produce a government: and this is the only mode in which governments have a right to arise, and the only principle on which they have a right to exist." [11] Therefore, "it is a perversion of terms to say that a charter gives rights. It operates by a contrary effect—that of taking rights away. Rights are inherently in all the inhabitants." [12]

The United Nation's Universal Declaration of Human Rights follows the same intrinsic logic, namely, the power behind any constitution or charter is derived from the legitimate authority of a state; the legitimate authority of a state, in turn, rests upon its mandate to promote and protect freedom, justice, and peace; this mandate requires that every state recognize the natural rights and the intrinsic dignity of every human being (because freedom, justice, and peace cannot be achieved without the protection of natural

---

paper.txt). When anti-Federalists prevailed and inserted the Bill of Rights into the U.S. Constitution, the Ninth Amendment was added to assure that natural rights would not be limited by a listing of rights in the Constitution.

[11] Thomas Paine, *The Rights of Man* (Stilwell, Kans.: Digireads.com Publishing, 2007), p. 29.

[12] Ibid., p. 115.

rights).[13] If any state fails to protect the natural rights of human beings, that state loses its legitimacy and its right to govern and can be legitimately rebelled against in the interest of justice, peace, and freedom. The United Nation's Universal Declaration phrases this reasoning as follows:

> Whereas recognition of the inherent dignity and of the equal and inalienable rights of all members of the human family is the foundation of freedom, justice and peace in the world,
>
> Whereas disregard and contempt for human rights have resulted in barbarous acts which have outraged the conscience of mankind, and the advent of a world in which human beings shall enjoy freedom of speech and belief and freedom from fear and want has been proclaimed as the highest aspiration of the common people,
>
> Whereas it is essential, if man is not to be compelled to have recourse, as a last resort, to rebellion against tyranny and oppression, that human rights should be protected by the rule of law.[14]

Why is this important? Because justices in the United States believe that their duty is to uphold the Constitution; but if they do not understand that the authority of the Constitution itself rests upon the inalienable natural rights of *all* human beings, then they not only undermine the Constitution, which they are sworn to uphold, but also turn themselves into wielders of arbitrary power. Regrettably, this misuse of power occurred in both the *Dred Scott* decision and in

---

[13] The United Nations Universal Declaration specifies these natural rights (irrespective of any constitution or political domain) as follows: "Everyone has the right to life, liberty and security of person" (Article 3). The Universal Declaration goes on to specify these three natural rights in subsequent articles (see United Nations, The Universal Declaration of Human Rights, December 10, 1948, www.un.org/en/documents/udhr/index.shtml).

[14] United Nations Universal Declaration, Preamble.

the *Roe v. Wade* decision (and its subsequent interpretation in cases such as *Planned Parenthood of Southeastern Pennsylvania v. Robert P. Casey*).[15]

The Dred Scott *Decision*

Let us first examine the *Dred Scott* decision of the U.S. Supreme Court.[16] Recall that las Casas used Principle 6 (principle of full human potential) to defend the Indian people from enslavement and murder against Sepúlveda and the Spanish court long before the abortion issue was awakened by the U.S. Supreme Court in *Roe v. Wade*. Now we see another striking parallel between the issue of slavery and the issue of abortion, this time with respect to natural rights, which arises out of the U.S. Supreme Court's forgetfulness (or perhaps culpable neglect) of its sworn duty to protect the natural rights of all human beings so that the Constitution may be justly administered and the Court's legitimate authority maintained. Consider these opening words in the 1857 decision of the Supreme Court:

> The question is simply this: Can a negro, whose ancestors were imported into this country, and sold as slaves, become a member of the political community formed and brought into existence by the *Constitution* of the United States, and as such *become entitled* to all the rights, and privileges, and immunities, guarantied *by that instrument* to the citizen? . . .
>
> The words "people of the United States" and "citizens" are synonymous terms, and mean the same thing. They both describe the political body who . . . form the *sovereignty*, and who hold the power and conduct the Government through their representatives. . . . The question before us is,

[15] See *Planned Parenthood v. Casey*, 505 U.S. 833 (1992).
[16] *Dred Scott v. Sanford*, [1] 60 U.S. (How. 19) 393 (1857).

whether the class of persons described in the plea in abate-
ment [people of African ancestry] compose a *portion of this
people*, and are constituent *members of this sovereignty?* We
think they are not, and that they are not included, and were
not intended to be included, under the word "citizens" in
the *Constitution*, and can therefore claim none of the rights
and privileges which that instrument provides for and secures
to *citizens of the United States*. On the contrary, they were at
that time considered as a *subordinate and inferior class of beings*,
who had been *subjugated by the dominant race*, and, whether
emancipated or not, yet remained subject to their authority, and *had no rights or privileges but such as those who held the
power and the Government might choose to grant them*.[17] (Italics
mine.)

Notice the following three violations of two of the ten
universal principles. First, the justices of the Supreme Court
overtly violated las Casas' principle that all human beings
be valued on the basis of their full human potential. They
declared people of African descent to be "a subordinate and
inferior class of beings", knowing full well that many in
this "class of beings" were not only capable of being educated, but also of being among the most articulate, moral,
spiritual, and naturally intelligent people in the country.[18]
Nevertheless, they *chose* not to judge this "class of beings"
according to their full potential, but rather on the basis that
their "ancestors were imported into this country, and sold
as slaves". Notice that this choice led to a violation of the

[17] Ibid.
[18] Frederick Douglass, a very prominent African American, not only owned
his own newspaper, but was also well known in both the North and South
for his writings on emancipation, rights, and women's suffrage. He defended
the Constitution of the United States (contrary to other abolitionists) as being
antislavery. The majority of slave owners were well aware that people of
African descent were not only educable, but also highly moral and spiritual,
and used them as tutors for their children.

principle of nonmaleficence (Principle 4)—that is, to the continued and unjustifiable enslavement (and maltreatment and even murder) of a large group of people.

Secondly, notice that the Supreme Court never mentions or even implies the existence of natural rights. The justices thought that their duty was not to defend the natural rights of human beings, but only to determine whether this class of human beings had *constitutional* (extrinsic) rights entitling them to legitimate citizenship in the United States:

> The question is simply this: Can a negro, whose ancestors were imported into this country, and sold as slaves, become a member of the political community formed and brought into existence by the *Constitution* of the United States, and as such *become entitled* to all the rights, and privileges, and immunities, guarantied *by that instrument* to the citizen?

Notice that the justices were either unaware of natural rights or simply assumed that people of African descent did not have natural rights (because they were considered subordinate and inferior). In either case, the decision violated one of the ten universal principles. If the justices were unaware of natural rights, then their ignorance led them to a gross violation of the principle of nonmaleficence. If they were aware of natural rights and judged people of African descent to be inferior, then they violated las Casas' principle, which, in turn, led them to a violation of the principle of nonmaleficence. This led to one of the greatest disgraces in our nation's history.

Thirdly, the justices assumed that all rights are derived from the Constitution and that constitutional rights belong only to "citizens". Notice that the justices believed that they had the authority to declare who had the right to life, liberty, and property ownership by declaring who was a citizen. Since they seem to have been unaware of the existence of natural rights, and believed themselves to be bound only to the defense of constitutionally declared rights, the power to declare citizenship became the power to declare who had a fundamental right to liberty. Thus, the justices believed they had the power to declare that certain human beings did *not* have a right to liberty. When they made their authority absolute, not bound to the constraints of natural rights, they made the decision that

> [w]e think [people of African descent] are not [citizens], and that they are not included, and were not intended to be included, under the word "citizens" in the Constitution, and can therefore claim none of the rights and privileges which that instrument provides for and secures to citizens of the United States. . . . [Therefore, they] remained subject to [the] authority [of the dominant race], and had no rights or privileges but such as those who held the power and the Government might choose to grant them.

The abolitionist movement, the Emancipation Proclamation, the discourses of Abraham Lincoln, and the Civil War (and its aftermath) concretely revealed the many errors of the Supreme Court's reasoning. The consequences were so terrible that one might think the Court would be careful not to make the same mistake again; yet it has decidedly done this in the *Roe v. Wade* decision.

The Roe v. Wade *Decision*

There are three salient passages that explain the Court's rationale in *Roe v. Wade*:

> If this suggestion of personhood is established, the appellant's case, of course, collapses, for the fetus' right to life

would then be guaranteed specifically by the Amendment. The appellant conceded as much on reargument. On the other hand, the appellee conceded on reargument that no case could be cited that holds that a fetus is a person within the meaning of the Fourteenth Amendment....

All this [the exclusively postnatal use of "person" in the Constitution and related precedents], together with our observation, supra, that throughout the major portion of the 19th century prevailing legal abortion practices were far freer than they are today, persuades us that the word "person," as used in the Fourteenth Amendment, does not include the unborn. (Section IX.A)

Texas urges that, apart from the Fourteenth Amendment, life begins at conception and is present throughout pregnancy, and that, therefore, the State has a compelling interest in protecting that life from and after conception. We need not resolve the difficult question of when life begins. When those trained in the respective disciplines of medicine, philosophy, and theology are unable to arrive at any consensus, the judiciary, at this point in the development of man's knowledge, is not in a position to speculate as to the answer. (Section IX.B)

This reasoning of the majority is logically fallacious (violating Principles 1–3), completely ignores the natural rights of prenatal human beings (violating Principle 7), does not assess human life according to its full potential (violating Principle 6), and, as a consequence, sanctions a serious violation of the principle of nonmaleficence (Principle 4, the bedrock of all ethics). In short, it abrogates just about every principle of humaneness and civility and cannot be considered anything better than a disaster in the history of civilization.

Let us take a closer look at the majority's reasoning. First, notice the uncanny resemblance between the *Roe v. Wade* decision and the *Dred Scott* decision with respect to the forgetfulness (or perhaps culpable neglect) of *natural* rights. In this case, the majority fixed its attention solely upon discovering the *constitutional* rights of the fetus. Recall that natural rights are the ground and purpose of all governmental authority (including the courts'),[19] which makes the *first* purpose of every court the protection of natural rights.[20] This, in turn, legitimizes its authority to interpret statutory law and adjudicate disputes. Locke and Jefferson realized that this first duty of the judiciary could also prevent a tyranny of the majority, where 51% of the people could order the execution of 49% of the people by a vote or by arbitrary statutory prescription. Votes and statutory prescriptions are not infallible. What makes them legitimate is their operation within the contours of the natural rights of all persons. Thus, a majority cannot vote out the natural rights of a minority, for such a vote would be illegitimate because it negates the ground and purpose of the governmental authority through which the vote originated.

---

[19] See the above citations by Francisco Suarez, John Locke, Thomas Jefferson, and Thomas Paine.

[20] Some strict constructionists might argue that it is not the purpose of the judicial branch to adjudicate issues of natural rights, and that natural law and natural rights are matters for the legislature to debate and determine. In this view, civil law reflects natural law and natural rights to the extent that the legislature properly formulates laws. If the law fails to protect natural rights, it is the responsibility of the legislature to revise its laws accordingly.

This strict constructionist view misses the point about natural rights. Recall from the above discussion of the United Nation's Universal Declaration of Human Rights that the legitimacy of the *state itself* rests upon the recognition and protection of inalienable natural rights. Therefore, the protection of such rights is not just the responsibility of the legislative branch, but rather, the responsibility of the *state itself*, which includes every branch of government and every citizen. In the fullest meaning of the Universal Declaration, the protection of natural rights is the responsibility of every individual *irrespective of citizenship* in any state. The judicial branch of any state does not have the right to circumscribe its responsibility to recognize and protect natural rights—doing so would automatically undermine its legitimacy and authority.

When the majority narrowed the criterion for the protection of unborn life to whether such life was protected under the Constitution alone, it abdicated its first duty to protect natural rights. In so doing, it undermined its own authority, which delegitimized its ruling. The majority might insist that it has the authority, but inasmuch as its actions undermine its own authority, such insistence is empty.

The idea of a natural right is to preserve life, not to kill it; and a constitutional right cannot supersede the natural right to life. The whole point of natural rights is that they cannot be superseded by the power of the state. Thus, the state cannot allow an initiative to come forward to permit the killing of people who are over 6 feet tall and weigh over 185 pounds, because they consume too many resources. Persons fitting this description have natural rights that cannot be superseded by contrary constitutional rights, court decisions, plebiscites, statutory prescriptions, etc.

The Supreme Court majority did not stop there. It used its spurious distinction between "person" and "human being" to "justify" focusing on constitutional rights alone. By asserting that constitutional rights belong only to persons, and that persons are not *every* human being, the majority tried to form a rationale that would allow them to legitimize abortion on the basis of whether fetuses were considered persons in the Constitution.

Notice that the majority has made a distinction between the human life of the fetus and the personhood of the fetus, implying that there is some difference between the two, but *never justifying* it (see above p. 63 passage number one *Roe v. Wade*, Section IX.A). All we know from the majority is that it considers a living human fetus to be distinct from a person, that it does not consider all human beings to be persons, and that persons are the only ones guaranteed protection under the Constitution. We are not told why *any* particular human life would *not* be considered a person. Recall from the discussion in Principle 4 that this idea of merely legal personhood is highly unusual and does not conform with the linguistic history of personhood, the ontological definition of personhood, or the ethical definition of personhood.

At this juncture, the majority shifted its burden of proof to a much easier bar to reach. Instead of justifying why a human life would *not* be considered a person, which is a burden of proof that the majority must meet in order to prevent a violation of the principles of natural rights and nonmaleficence, it shifted its burden to justifying why human life *should* be considered a person. Obviously, this is an easier burden of proof to meet because one does not have to assume from the beginning that all human beings are persons.

According to this logic, the Court would not have to show, for example, why people who are taller than six foot five should *not* be considered persons, and deserving of protection under the law; it would only have to show why people who are taller than six feet *should* be considered persons. If they cannot find any proof for this in the Constitution, then the way would be clear to authorizing the death of these people, who obviously consume too many resources. Again, the Court would not have to show why human beings born in other countries should *not* be considered persons; it would only have to show why these foreign human beings who are consuming American resources *should* be considered persons. Is there a use of the word "person" in the Constitution that specifically applies to foreign human beings? Uh-oh.

According to this logic, the Court could sanction any penalty for any particular group of human beings simply because the Constitution did not explicitly mention them as "persons". Notice how this same reasoning is used in the *Dred Scott* decision, where the Court did not believe that it had a burden to prove why black human beings should *not* be considered citizens, but only why black human beings *should* be considered citizens. When it could find no such proof in the Constitution, it allowed them to be enslaved. The fallacious and harmful logic of the *Dred Scott* and *Roe v. Wade* decisions are identical.

We may now see a similar strategy by the Court in both the *Dred Scott* decision and the *Roe v. Wade* decision to use its spurious distinctions to navigate around the nagging problem of natural rights, and to focus on constitutional rights alone. Recall that just as the Court in the *Dred Scott* decision distinguished "citizens" from "all human beings", the majority in *Roe v. Wade* distinguished "persons" from "all human beings". Now watch the remarkably similar "sleight of hand". After the distinctions were made, both Court decisions declared that its only responsibility was to determine whether people of African descent or unborn human beings were citizens or persons according to the Constitution. It would have been a successful strategy were it not for the fact that natural rights cannot be superseded by constitutional rights, and that natural rights pertain to all human beings, and not merely to "citizens" and "persons" as the Court arbitrarily defines them.

It must be emphasized in the arena of *natural* rights that all attempts to distinguish "citizens" or "persons", or any other specially selected category, from "human beings" are specious and dangerous because they are intended to shift the focus from "*all* human beings" to only certain *kinds* of human beings. Though the Supreme Court has the justifiable power to determine who has extrinsic rights, such as the right to vote, it has no authority or power to refuse protection of natural rights to any human being under its jurisdiction. The Court cannot sanction the execution of an illegal immigrant merely because that human being is not a citizen. It cannot sanction enslaving, torturing, or taking away the legitimately obtained property of such a noncitizen, because the Court has a primary duty and responsibility to protect the *natural* rights of *all* human beings within its jurisdiction—failure to do so undermines its purpose, and with it the entire legal system.

Incredibly, the unusual logic of the *Roe v. Wade* decision goes even further. Not only did the majority abdicate its responsibility to protect the *natural rights* of all human beings within its jurisdiction; not only did it shift its burden of proof from showing why human beings should *not* be considered persons, deserving of protection under the law, to why human beings *should* be considered persons—it made a blatant logical error to bring its fallacious reasoning to its fallacious conclusion. Following the example of the majority in the *Dred Scott* decision, the majority in *Roe v. Wade* committed the fallacy of construing silence to be valid evidence to rule out not only the natural rights but also the constitutional rights of human beings. Recall the majority's conclusion in this regard (see p. 63 above):

> All this [the exclusively postnatal use of "person" in the Constitution and related precedents], together with our observation, supra, that throughout the major portion of the 19th century prevailing legal abortion practices were far freer than they are today, persuades us that the word "person," as used in the Fourteenth Amendment, does not include the unborn.

Notice here that the majority searched the Constitution (particularly the Fourteenth Amendment) to find any prenatal use of "person", and when it found the Constitution silent on this topic, it interpreted that silence to mean that the Constitution did *not* intend to include the unborn ("persuades us that the word 'person,' as used in the Fourteenth Amendment, does not include the unborn"). First and foremost, this reasoning goes against the centuries-old dictum, which has been embraced by American jurists from the beginning of this country, that silence has little probative value,[21] because it literally provides no evidence in the affirmative or the negative. To construe silence to mean anything other than "nothing" is a disingenuous leaping non sequitur.

This legal dictum mirrors a well-known logical fallacy: negating the antecedent. The form of this fallacy is as follows: "If A, then B. Not A. Therefore, not B." Here is an example of this. "If there is rain outside, then there must be water vapor outside. But there is no rain outside. Therefore, there is no water vapor outside." This is a fallacious conclusion. Even though it is true that if there is rain, there must be water vapor, it does not follow that if there is *no* rain, there is *no* water vapor. It could be a humid day without rain. Now let us examine the majority's reasoning in *Roe v. Wade*. It is evidently true that if there is mention of unborn life in the Constitution, then the Constitution intended to include unborn life within the scope of "persons deserving protection under the law". However, one cannot deduce from this that *non* mention of unborn life in the Constitution implies that the Constitution did *not* intend to include unborn life within the scope of persons deserving protection under the law.

<hr />

[21] Michael M. Martin, Daniel J. Capra, and Faust F. Rossi, *New York Evidence Handbook: Rules, Theory, and Practice*, 2nd ed. (New York: Aspen Publishers, 2003), p. 181.

The logical fallacy and injustice of this way of thinking in both *Roe v. Wade* and the *Dred Scott* decisions might be illustrated with the following example. Let us suppose that we discover a tribe of people with full human genomes in a hidden valley in the United States. Let us further suppose that these people had not yet fully developed computer and energy technologies similar to our own, and that the question arose about whether they were guaranteed the right of protection under the law. Now, in the Constitution, the word "person" is not explicitly used of less developed tribes in hidden valleys. Does this mean that the Constitution does not protect this group of people? Does it also mean therefore that the state is not obliged to protect this group of people? Carrying the analogy further, if we forget about natural rights of beings of human origin, could the courts therefore permit the wholesale slaughter of the tribe?

It is of little consequence that the people in our example have already been born, because the key issue is that they have not achieved their full potential and this fact could be judged to make their personhood ambiguous. This supposed ambiguity about their personhood, in turn, allows them to fall through the proverbial "constitutional cracks", because the Constitution does not use "person" to refer specifically to primitive tribal members living in hidden valleys. According to the logic of the majority in *Roe v. Wade*, the courts are not responsible for protecting the lives of these tribal people, and so if these people should ever impinge upon the privacy rights of "real" citizens living close to the hidden valley, those citizens would be able to terminate them without fearing recourse from the law.

Why did the majority in both *Roe v. Wade* and *Dred Scott* violate a centuries-old prohibition of construing silence to be valid evidence? It seems that they did not want to stop at anything preventing them from reaching their predetermined conclusions. They wanted these conclusions so much that they were willing not only to jeopardize millions of human beings and risk the undermining of all prescriptive laws in the legal system, but also to risk centuries of criticism when their reasoning was exposed as fallacious and in violation of their own rules of evidence.

Unjust Laws and Civil Disobedience

How can we as U.S. citizens respond to this? We want to respect the highest court in the land, but how can we do this when the Court has lost its respectability, when it has ignored the natural rights of human beings, when it has failed to show why *every* human being should *not* be considered a person, when it has violated its own rules of evidence, and most importantly, when it has so grossly violated the principle of nonmaleficence? Do citizens have to obey such decisions which are rightfully designated as "unjust laws"? History is replete with examples of great thinkers and movements who have resoundingly responded no. This "no" stands at the center of civil disobedience which advocates refusing to obey an unjust law while trying to change that law by peaceful means. This idea goes back to Saint Augustine, who declared that "an unjust law is no law at all." [22] What Augustine noticed was that even though an unjust law has the *extrinsic* authority of being mandated by governmental power, it has no *intrinsic* authority because law in general has as its sole purpose the service of justice. Any law which undermines its own purpose negates itself—it is no law at all.

[22] Augustine, *On Free Choice of the Will*, bk. 1, sec. 5.

Virtually every political philosopher has advocated the nonbinding force of such unjust laws and have further advocated resistance and civil disobedience. A few such advocates have been Saint Thomas Aquinas,[23] Francisco Suarez,[24] John Locke,[25] Thomas Jefferson,[26] Edmund Burke,[27] Mahatma Gandhi,[28] and Martin Luther

[23] "Laws may be unjust in two ways: first, by being contrary to human good, through being opposed to the things mentioned above—either in respect of the end, as when an authority imposes on his subjects burdensome laws, conducive, not to the common good, but rather to his own cupidity or vainglory—or in respect of the author, as when a man makes a law that goes beyond the power committed to him—or in respect of the form, as when burdens are imposed unequally on the community, although with a view to the common good. The like are acts of violence rather than laws; because, as Augustine says (*De Lib.* Arb. i, 5), 'a law that is not just, seems to be no law at all'" (Aquinas, *Summa Theologica*, I–II, q. 96, a. 4).

[24] "[F]or a law to be genuine law, it must ... be just and reasonable, because an unjust law is not law" (Suarez, *De Legibus*, 3.22.1.6, 84). He explicates this principle as follows: "[T]he human lawmaker ... does not have the power to bind through unjust laws, and, therefore, were he to command unjust things, such prescriptions would not be law, because they have neither the force nor the validity necessary to bind" (*De Legibus*, 1.9.4.2, 6).

[25] "As usurpation is the exercise of power, which another hath a right to; so tyranny is the exercise of power beyond right, which no body can have a right to. And this is making use of the power any one has in his hands, not for the good of those who are under it, but for his own private separate advantage. When the governor, however intitled, makes not the law, but his will, the rule; and his commands and actions are not directed to the preservation of the properties of his people, but the satisfaction of his own ambition, revenge, covetousness, or any other irregular passion ..." (Locke, *Second Treatise*, chap. 18, sec. 199, p. 54).

[26] A saying popularly attributed to Thomas Jefferson is, "If a law is unjust, a man is not only right to disobey it, he is obligated to do so."

[27] "It is not what a lawyer tells me I may do; but what humanity, reason, and justice tell me I ought to do" (Edmund Burke, *Second Speech on Conciliation*, 1775).

[28] "Civil Disobedience ... becomes a sacred duty when the state has become lawless or, which is the same thing, corrupt. And a citizen who barters with such a state shares its corruption or lawlessness" (Mahatma Gandhi) in D. G. Tendulkar, *Mahatma Life of Mohandas Karamohand Gandhi*, vol. 2 of 8 (Ahmedabad, India: Navajivan Publishing House, 1960, 2nd ed.), p. 76.

King, Jr.[29] Perhaps the most detailed expositor of this doctrine was Henry David Thoreau, who wrote in his essay *On the Duty of Civil Disobedience*:

> If the injustice is part of the necessary friction of the machine of government, let it go, let it go: perchance it will wear smooth—certainly the machine will wear out. If the injustice has a spring, or a pulley, or a rope, or a crank, exclusively for itself, then perhaps you may consider whether the remedy will not be worse than the evil; but if it is of such a nature that it requires you to be the agent of injustice to another, then, I say, break the law. Let your life be a counter friction to stop the machine. What I have to do is to see, at any rate, that I do not lend myself to the wrong which I condemn.[30]

In the case of the severe injustice meted out daily to unborn babies, tolerance is not justifiable. We cannot and should not accept the decision of the majority out of respect for the Court. When governmental authorities wield power arbitrarily and unjustly, they undermine their decisions, their respectability, and their authority. Even though such authorities possess civil power, the unjust use of that power undermines its legitimacy. The majority's violation of the principles of nonmaleficence and natural rights (justice) and the fallacious arguments used to defend these indignities do not arise out of the "necessary friction of the machine of

[29] "One may well ask: 'How can you advocate breaking some laws and obeying others?' The answer lies in the fact that there are two types of laws: just and unjust. I would be the first to advocate obeying just laws. One has not only a legal but a moral responsibility to obey just laws. Conversely, one has a moral responsibility to disobey unjust laws. I would agree with St. Augustine that 'an unjust law is no law at all'" (Letter from Birmingham Jail, April 16, 1963).

[30] Henry David Thoreau, *On the Duty of Civil Disobedience* (London: Simple Life Press, 1903), p. 39.

government"; they are severe injustices which are unnecessary for the function of government and therefore cannot be tolerated. In keeping with the mind and heart of Aquinas, Suarez, Locke, Jefferson, Burke, Gandhi, King, and Thoreau, this legal decision should be resisted, and we must become "a counter friction to stop the machine".

Principle 8: The Principle of the Fundamentality of Rights

The more fundamental right is the one which is necessary for the possibility of the other; where there is a conflict, we should resolve in favor of the more fundamental right.

We begin our discussion once again with the originator of natural rights: the Spanish Jesuit Francisco Suarez. Recall that Suarez believed that the ground and aim of law itself is "the due preservation and natural perfection or happiness of human nature",[31] from which he derives his theory of rights. We can see the faint outline of Jefferson's three inalienable rights in this passage—Suarez's right to self-preservation corresponding to Jefferson's right to life, Suarez's right to the natural perfection of human nature corresponding to Jefferson's right to liberty,[32] and Suarez's right to happiness corresponding to Jefferson's right to the pursuit of happiness.

In another part of *De Legibus*, Suarez includes property within the notion of natural rights: "[rights are] a kind of moral power which every man has, either over his own

---

[31] Suarez, *De Legibus*, 3.2.7.7, 118.

[32] Jefferson's Enlightenment notion of liberty was unknown to the Scholastic era in which Suarez lived. The closest Suarez could have come to such a notion of liberty, given the conceptual structures of Scholasticism, was something akin to "natural perfection ... of human nature".

property or with respect to that which is due to him." [33]
Though there is an *implicit* priority of the right to self-preservation over the right to the natural perfection of human nature, there is no *explicit* prioritization of life over liberty and liberty over happiness and property.

The prioritization of rights becomes clearer in John Locke's *Second Treatise on Government* where he places the right to life ahead of the right to liberty, and the right to liberty ahead of the right to property:

> Man being born, as has been proved, with a title to perfect freedom, and an uncontrolled enjoyment of all the rights and privileges of the law of nature, equally with any other man, or number of men in the world, hath by nature a power, . . . to preserve his property, that is, his life, liberty and estate, against the injuries and attempts of other men. [34]

As we saw above, the prioritization becomes even clearer with Thomas Jefferson, who changes Locke's right of prop erty ownership back to Suarez's right to happiness: "We hold these truths to be self-evident, that all men are created equal, that they are endowed by their Creator with certain unalienable Rights, that among these are Life, Liberty and the pursuit of Happiness."

Suarez, Locke, and Jefferson do not attempt to justify the prioritization of rights in an explicitly formal way; yet they seem to assume that life precedes liberty, and liberty precedes other natural rights. Why did they assume that this truth was evident? The answer probably lies in their implicit application of a well-known technique in philosophy termed "the condition necessary for the possibility of _____". Recall from Principle 3 that there are two kinds of objective evidence: a

---

[33] Suarez, *De Legibus*, 1.2.5.
[34] Locke, *Second Treatise*, p. 46.

posteriori evidence (sensorial evidence), and a priori evidence (evidence from necessity). As will be seen, this particular technique is used to discover a priori evidence and can be used in metaphysics, physics, political theory, and ethics. For example, in metaphysics, if existence is a condition necessary for the possibility of time, then existence must be a more fundamental reality than time. In physics, if space and energy are conditions necessary for the possibility of locomotion, then space and energy are more fundamental realities than locomotion.

The same holds true for rights theory. If the right to life is a condition necessary for the possibility of the right to liberty (but not vice versa), then the right to life must be more fundamental than the right to liberty. Similarly, if the right to liberty is a condition necessary for the possibility of the right to own property, then the right to liberty must be more fundamental than the right to own property.

Now, the right to life is obviously a condition necessary for the *possibility* of the right to liberty because if one is dead, one's right to liberty is truly a moot question. Similarly, the right to liberty must also be a condition necessary for the possibility of the right to own property, for if person A can own another person (B), then person A owns all of person B's property along with him. Person B's property rights are truly a moot question. Therefore, it can be said *objectively* (that is, by the criterion of necessity which is not a mere matter of subjective assertion) that the right to life is more fundamental than the right to liberty and the right to property, and the right to liberty is more fundamental than the right to property.

This principle is important in the resolution of rights conflicts, because it gives an *objective* (necessary) way of resolving those conflicts. In order to respect not only the natural rights of human beings, but also the fundamentality of those natural rights, we must hold the more fundamental right to be the more important right in resolving rights conflicts. This is the only way to respect the principle of nonmaleficence, because a violation of a more fundamental right leads to a greater harm than the violation of a less fundamental right. For example, if a court must choose between person X's right to life and person Y's right to liberty, the court is obligated to act in favor of person X's right to life, because his death would be a greater harm than person Y's loss of liberty. Thus, the principle of the fundamentality of rights is a necessary extension of the principle of nonmaleficence.

Now, if we have an objective criterion to assess which right is more fundamental, and we must uphold the fundamentality of rights in order to uphold the principle of nonmaleficence, a court (and anyone else, for that matter) is obligated to abide by this objective principle. Recall that an objective principle protects us from the arbitrariness of merely subjective claims, and that the principle of nonmaleficence is the most fundamental ethical principle, without which ethics has nothing to build on. Thus, if we are going to protect the most fundamental ethical principle, we must protect against the arbitrariness of subjective assertions in its application, which means that we must utilize an objective criterion (such as a necessary criterion) to apply it.

As might now be obvious, the U.S. Supreme Court failed to apply this objective criterion of fundamentality to two major issues: slavery and abortion. Let us begin with the *Dred Scott* decision. Recall from the above explication of that case, that the U.S. Supreme Court had to make a decision about which rights were more fundamental—the liberty rights of black people or the property rights of white people. If the Court had used the objective criterion of "the condition necessary for the possibility of _____", it would have had to resolve this conflict in favor of black people's liberty rights, because liberty rights are a condition necessary for the possibility of property rights. Doing so would have protected them against doing greater harm to one party over another. We saw above that the Court acted in the opposite way, attempting to justify its decision by asserting that, since the Constitution did not explicitly include black people, the Founding Fathers intended to exclude them. This led to the sanctioning of a much greater harm.

We may now return to the majority's reasoning in the *Roe v. Wade* decision. In some ways, it is a more egregious violation of the principle of the fundamentality of rights than the *Dred Scott* decision, because it justifies a violation of the indisputably primary right to life. The majority in the *Roe v. Wade* decision was far bolder than the Court in the *Dred Scott* decision because the majority in *Roe v. Wade* explicitly proclaimed its prioritization of the woman's right to privacy (liberty) over the unborn human being's right to life:

> State criminal abortion laws, like those involved here, that except from criminality only a life-saving procedure on the mother's behalf without regard to the stage of her pregnancy and other interests involved violate the Due Process Clause of the Fourteenth Amendment, which protects against state action the right to privacy, including a woman's qualified right to terminate her pregnancy. Though the State cannot override that right . . . (*Roe v. Wade*, 3)

The majority implies here that it is permissible to violate a more fundamental right in order to protect a less fundamental one, which forces it to justify a greater violation of the principle of nonmaleficence.[35] We have already seen

[35] Even though the majority did not state that they were allowing a less fundamental right to "trump" a more fundamental one, they did this by implication and caused an equivalent harm. It would be sad to think that

how the majority used the same fallacious reasoning as that used in the *Dred Scott* decision—looking for an explicit reference to fetal personhood in the Constitution, and upon not finding it, concluding that the Constitution did not consider fetuses to be persons. The majority had to use this kind of fallacious argument in attempting to justify its decision, because its decision went against the objective (necessary) criterion of the fundamentality of rights.

Some advocates of abortion, in an attempt to salvage the Court's reasoning, have suggested that since women have reached full actualization of their human potential while fetuses have not, women's rights should be preferred over fetal rights. This is an obvious violation of the principle of full human potential, which was violated by Sepulveda in his attempt to justify the enslavement and murder of Indians in the New World and was also violated by the Court in the *Dred Scott* decision to justify the enslaving of people of African descent. The violation of this principle is equally unjust when applied to unborn human life. As noted above, failure to value human beings according to their full potential leads to serious violations of the principle of nonmaleficence and the undermining of ethics and governmental authority, and so the incomplete achievement of full human potential cannot be used to justify favoring the right to liberty over the right to life.

When some of these advocates learn that the "full actualization" justification is specious and harmful, they move to the criterion of clarity to justify the Court's decision, noting that women can be seen to be human, more clearly than human fetuses. This supposedly justifies why women's less fundamental privacy rights should be given priority over

they did not even recognize the problem because this would indicate remarkable naiveté on the part of the highest court in the land.

the more fundamental life rights of fetuses. Recall from Principle 3 (concerning objective evidence) that clarity is a merely *subjective* criterion that depends on the perspective and acuity of particular observers.

For example, Einstein considered the special theory of relativity to be clear, but many of my students do not. This does not indicate an objective problem with the special theory of relativity, but rather with the intellectual preparedness of my students, which is a subjective rather than an objective problem. Similarly, an embryologist who observes first-trimester fetuses on a daily basis with ultrasound technology and fetoscopy (intrauterine photographic technology) may consider their humanity to be as clearly evident as that of women's. Again, there is no problem with objectively establishing the humanity of the fetus with a DNA sequencer; the only problem is some people's lack of perspective, technology, or intellectual preparedness (a subjective problem). It is completely unwarranted to advocate the negation of the objective principle of fundamentality in order to accommodate subjective limitations in perspective, technology, and intellectual preparedness. Therefore, the objective fundamentality of rights should not be compromised, and the primacy of the life rights of the unborn should be restored.

Principle 9: The Principle of Limits to Freedom

One person's (or group's) freedoms cannot impose undue burdens upon other persons (or groups).

This principle is an extension of natural rights. Francisco Suarez did not mention it because the Scholasticism of his day had not developed an Enlightenment view of freedom or liberty. However, Locke was aware of this notion of freedom and put it in a very important place in his theory of rights. Even though he believed that liberty should be given the widest possible space in which to operate, he hastened to add in several critical passages in the *Second Treatise on Government* that one person's liberty stops where another person's rights begin. In one such passage he notes:

But though this be a state of liberty, yet it is not a state of licence; though man in that state have an uncontrollable liberty to dispose of his person or possessions, yet he has not liberty to destroy himself, or so much as any creature in his possession, but where some nobler use than its bare preservation calls for it. The state of Nature has a law of Nature to govern it, which obliges every one; and reason, which is that law, teaches all mankind who will but consult it, that being all equal and independent, no one ought to harm another in his life, health, liberty or possessions.[36]

Baron de Montesquieu (1689–1755) interprets rights as liberties more than powers inherent in an individual human being. Even though, like Locke, Montesquieu believed that liberty should be as uncontrolled as possible in every human being, he also believed that one person's liberties cannot harm or threaten the safety of other persons, and so he writes: "The political liberty of the subject is a tranquility of mind arising from the opinion each person has of his safety. In order to have this liberty, it is requisite the government be so constituted as one man need not be afraid of another."[37] Notice that Montesquieu not only believes that one person's liberties should not cause undue burdens

[36] Locke, *Second Treatise*, p. 9.
[37] Baron de Montesquieu, *The Spirit of the Laws* (New York: Hafner Publishing, 1949), p. 153. See also bk. II, sections 3–6, pp. 150–62.

on another person, but also that the government is responsible for assuring that this does not occur. He even advocates that governments be constituted according to this principle, and so he develops the theory of checks and balances among the branches of government that influenced our Founding Fathers and became the bedrock of our Constitution.

Inasmuch as all legitimate governments are responsible for actualizing this principle, we may infer that governments should not grant freedoms to one group of individuals that will likely create undue burdens for others or threaten the safety of others.

This particular principle is applicable to the life issues in a variety of ways. First, with respect to the abortion issue, there is the obvious problem that in order to grant a new freedom to mothers to abort their fetuses, the courts have to impose an undue burden on these unborn children to die. Even though these victims cannot speak for themselves, they still have natural rights, which belong to them in themselves and are present by virtue of their human existence alone. Being able to speak for themselves is not a necessary condition of their natural right to life. Again, the *Roe v. Wade* decision has violated a key universal principle: imposing undue burdens on one group in order to give greater freedom to another group.

Recent attempts to pass euthanasia legislation also undermine this principle. "Active euthanasia" refers to taking the life of a patient by some active means, usually by a lethal injection or a lethal dose of medication given to the patient to take by himself, resulting in assisted suicide.

At first glance, one might think that this should not be a problem, because if somebody wants to commit suicide by means of a lethal dose of medication, it would seem to be his business. "Why should the state get involved in preventing this? Why not give people the option (freedom) to kill themselves or have themselves killed if they really want it?"

Recall that governments do not have the right simply to grant freedoms. They can only recognize freedoms when those freedoms do not impose an undue burden on other groups, and it is incumbent upon governments to do their due diligence in identifying any potential undue burdens that may arise in this process.

Now, on the surface, it does not seem that there are any groups that would experience undue burdens from granting certain individuals the freedom to kill themselves or have themselves killed; but this initial judgment is quite deceptive. When we look below the surface, we can see that giving an *option* for assisted suicide or lethal injection can create a large number of burdens to those who may be pressured to choose death when they really do not want it. This pressure can come from external parties who may purposely or accidentally suggest or propose assisted suicide. Let us examine just a few particularly vulnerable groups.

The first vulnerable group consists of persons who are likely to be pressured to commit assisted suicide by relatives or others who may have something to gain. This pressure cannot be exerted if the option for euthanasia does not exist. However, the moment it does exist, it leaves an opportunity for mal-intended relatives either subtly or blatantly to suggest this choice as the "responsible thing to do". "Your medical expenses sure are getting high", or "Your medical expenses are drawing down your net worth", or "You are depriving the world of medical resources which could be used for much better purposes" (that is, for people who would live longer). More subtle pressures can be exerted on potential victims, but the effect is the same: an undue "duty" to die

for one group of people that did not exist before the freedom for euthanasia was given to another much smaller group
of people. This pressure should be considered an *"undue
burden to die"* because the vast majority of people want to
live, and most of those who make suicide requests reverse
them when their pain and depression are treated properly.[38]

*A second group of potential victims are those with limited finan-
cial resources.* If the option for assisted-suicide does not exist,
these individuals will receive treatment either from Medi-
care, Medicaid, charities, insurance companies, or other
sources. However, if the option does exist, it may come to
pass that government and insurance agencies may choose to
curb payment for end-of-life treatments in favor of paying
for assisted-suicide, and if this occurs, people with limited
financial resources will suffer discrimination because they
will be pressured to avail themselves of it merely because of
their financial condition. This future has already come to
pass in the state of Oregon.[39]

---

[38] These pain and depression protocols are widely available in the United
States today. See, for example, Kathleen Foley and Herbert Hendin, eds.,
The Case against Assisted Suicide: For the Right to End-of-Life Care (Baltimore:
Johns Hopkins University Press, 2002), pp. 4–5, 227–28, 314–15, 330–31.
See also Kathleen Foley, "The Relationship of Pain and Symptom Manage-
ment to Patient Requests for Physician-Assisted Suicide", *Journal of Pain and
Symptom Management* 6 (1991): 290.

[39] After assisted-suicide had been legalized in Oregon, the *Seattle Times* reported
the story of one of its victims: "Barbara Wagner, a Lane County woman suffering from lung cancer, was turned down by the state's Oregon Health Plan
for a new drug called Tarceva. In a letter sent by a company that administers
one of the state's insurance plans, Wagner was informed of the 'physician aid in
dying' option that could include lethal prescriptions as well as visits to doctors
required to obtain the drugs. 'I was absolutely hurt that somebody could think
that way,' said Wagner. 'They won't pay for me to live but they will pay for me
to die'" (Hal Bernton, "Washington's Initiative 1000 is Modeled on Oregon's
Death with Dignity Act", *Seattle Times*, October 13, 2008).
   An account of another victim was reported by Fox News: "Some termi-
nally ill patients in Oregon who turned to their state for health care were

In addition to the direct victims of active euthanasia, there are also a myriad of potential indirect victims. *A third group would be those with low self-esteem who have no strong religious or philosophical beliefs against suicide.* Individuals with low self-esteem are predisposed to hear and receive the most negative suggestion made by an authority figure (such as a doctor). If a doctor gives a person with low self-esteem the choice between palliative care and euthanasia, that person may hear a subliminal message: "The doctor thinks I deserve to die. I'll take euthanasia." Such an individual is not psychologically free to "choose" euthanasia, and so the supposed "choice" becomes an implicit imposition. The large number of people suffering from low self-esteem within our culture manifests the potential harm.

A fourth group of potential victims includes those suffering from reversible depression, a state which is common, and commonly reversible, during terminal illness. The depression and anger that seems to be intrinsic to cases of terminal illness generally subsides or disappears altogether as depression is treated and patients move closer to death.[40] Obviously, we are "not ourselves" when we are upset or depressed.

---

denied treatment and offered doctor-assisted suicide instead, a proposal some experts have called a 'chilling' corruption of medical ethics. Since the spread of his prostate cancer, 53-year-old Randy Stroup of Dexter, Ore., has been in a fight for his life. Uninsured and unable to pay for expensive chemotherapy, he applied to Oregon's state-run health plan for help. Lane Individual Practice Association (LIPA), which administers the Oregon Health Plan in Lane County, responded to Stroup's request with a letter saying the state would not cover Stroup's pricey treatment, but would pay for the cost of physician-assisted suicide. 'It dropped my chin to the floor,' Stroup told FOX News. '[How could they] not pay for medication that would help my life, and yet offer to pay to end my life?'" (Dan Springer, "Oregon Offers Terminal Patients Doctor-Assisted Suicide Instead of Medical Care", Fox News, July 28, 2008).

[40] See Elizabeth Kubler-Ross, *On Death and Dying* (New York: Scribner Classics, 1997); and also Foley and Hendin, *Case against Assisted Suicide.*

The mood swings inherent to anger, and the hopelessness, emptiness, and bleakness associated with depression, can make us do what we otherwise would not. Terminal patients commonly report times when they would have "chosen" to die had euthanasia been legal, and expressed great relief that the "choice" had not been available, for they regained their desire to live and benefited greatly from continued life.[41]

A fifth group concerns stoic heroes. Such individuals loathe dependency and weakness and would rather die than admit either, preferring to "end it all while I'm still strong". Such an individual could easily "choose" euthanasia in the early stages of terminal illness, before any functional compromise, and die without consulting friends or family to "avoid burdening them". This, of course, would load the survivors with all the trauma of a suicide, while ignoring the possibility that the "hero" and his relatives and friends might together discover higher levels of purpose in life.

A sixth group are the victims of inadvertent cruelty. Perhaps a mother, given a terminal diagnosis and the option of palliation or death, turns to her daughter for advice. The daughter, not wishing to impose her values on her mother, says, "Choose whichever you think is right, Mom. We'll support whatever you want to do." The mother thinks, "That's all I mean to her!? She doesn't care if I live or die?! Then why go on? I'll end it all." What was intended to be supportive and nonjudgmental was construed as the ultimate rejection. Again, the option of assisted suicide can result in an unwelcome decision to die.

Each of these categories of victims represents ways in which "choice" becomes a form of "duty", "an available option" becomes "the only acceptable option". Large segments of our population are vulnerable to these mal-intended motives

---

[41] See the references in the previous note.

or mistaken interpretations. One need only look at the numbers of people who live through depression, low self-esteem, and stoic heroism to see the potential victims who might feel themselves compelled to cut short what could have been the most profound and constructive part of their lives, for themselves and for their loved ones. The potential victims far outnumber those who want to avail themselves of physician-assisted suicide.

We now return to our principle, that governments should not grant freedoms to one group of people that will impose undue burdens on other groups of people. The above analysis of these groups in the case of active euthanasia should alert every governmental authority to the violation not only of this principle, but also the principle of nonmaleficence. It is not sufficient for such authorities to say, "We are only acceding to the will of the majority who voted for this new freedom", because governments are responsible for preventing a "tyranny of the majority" Even if a majority of people want a new freedom to commit assisted suicide, the judiciary, in recognizing the possibility of intended and unintended victims, cannot permit this majority to oppress the minority with undue burdens. Such initiatives or referendums should not be permitted on the ballot for the same reason that a government would prohibit a ballot measure from the Ku Klux Klan advocating the persecution of various minorities. Such laws should be immediately reversed to prevent any further harm to intended and unintended victims.

IV.

FUNDAMENTAL PRINCIPLE OF IDENTITY AND CULTURE

The principle of beneficence (the Golden Rule) stands at the foundation of higher levels of human purpose, identity, and culture. It has the capacity to effect transformation of our self-image, strivings, happiness, and sense of success, quality of life, freedom, ethics, love, and the common good. It is perhaps the most powerful idea of human transformation and is a beacon of hope for individuals and the culture.

The placement of this principle at the end of this book is not meant to indicate diminished importance among the ten principles. Indeed, nothing could be further from the truth. It was my judgment that *minimalistic* principles of ethics and justice should be addressed first because the principle of beneficence presumes and depends on them. As will be seen, it is impossible to pursue the principle of beneficence without adherence to the principle of non-maleficence and its corollaries in ethics, justice, and rights. The principle of beneficence offers the potential to move beyond the minimum and to pursue the highest aspirations of the collective human spirit—what is most noble and most worthy of our creativity, energy, time, and sacrifices.

Principle 10: The Principle of Beneficence

Aim at optimal contribution to others and society.

The Golden Rule: Do unto others as you would have them do unto you.

The Golden Rule (the principle of beneficence) is distinct from the Silver Rule (the principle of nonmaleficence) in that the former is ethical maximalism ("Do good for others") while the latter is ethical minimalism ("Avoid harm to others"). The Golden Rule necessarily includes the Silver Rule because it would be difficult to pursue the good for others while harming them. However, the Golden Rule encompasses a much greater domain of activities than the Silver Rule because the goods that one can do for someone far exceed the harms which one needs to avoid. Thus, a Venn diagram would portray the Silver Rule as a very small circle within the much larger circle of the Golden Rule.

As noted in the discussion of the principle of nonmaleficence, virtually every religious tradition has some form of the Silver Rule, which is the foundation of all ethics and proscriptive law. The Old Testament has explicit references to the Silver Rule in both Tobit 4:15 ("What you hate, do not do to any one") and Sirach 31:15 ("Judge your neighbor's feelings by your own, and in every matter be thoughtful").

It seems that Jesus came on the scene in first-century Palestine and, without obvious precedent, formulated the most well-known version of the Golden Rule. By removing the "nots" from the Silver Rule, he transformed ethics from the *obligation* to avoid harm to the *aspiration* to optimize the good for one's neighbor. Jesus intended that the Silver Rule be included in his version of the Golden Rule, but he wanted moral or ethical life to be more than avoiding negative actions (a double negative)—he wanted a transformation of the human heart toward genuine love of one's neighbor. He desired that we see the unique dignity, goodness, lovability, and mystery in others and be moved not only to empathy, but also, through that empathy, to do the good for others as if we were doing the good for ourselves. He desired that we lose the distinction between ourselves and others in our pursuit of the good.[1]

The propagation of the Golden Rule, and Jesus' concomitant teaching on love, probably gave rise to more positive cultural transformation than any other single ethical teaching in history. Though history is replete with examples of leaders and cultures either ignoring or rejecting the Golden Rule, we can see its positive effects in the development of charitable relief for the poor (beginning in the first century), publicly accessible hospitals and educational institutions (since the time of Constantine), and the development of the justice theory, natural rights theory, economic rights theory, social justice theory, and international organizations to alleviate global poverty and injustice in the centuries thereafter.

The Golden Rule can provide a ground for personal identity and culture because it is the primary inspiration for higher levels of happiness and purpose in life. This may seem at first glance like an extraordinary claim, but a brief explanation of my theory of the four levels of happiness/ purpose will help to clarify it.[2] Bear in mind as we progress

[1] See Robert J. Spitzer, S.J., *Five Pillars of the Spiritual Life* (San Francisco: Ignatius Press, 2008), chapter 3. I have also completed a manuscript entitled *Jesus-Emmanuel* (to be published in 2012), which explains in great detail Jesus' understanding of love.

[2] This explanation is quite brief, but a much fuller explanation is given in Robert J. Spitzer, S.J., *Healing the Culture: A Commonsense Philosophy of Happiness, Freedom, and the Life Issues* (San Francisco: Ignatius Press, 2000), chapters 2–4.

through the levels that Level 3, the contributive identity, represents the Golden Rule.

Four Levels of Happiness

There is a large body of evidence supporting the theory of the four levels of happiness (or purpose) in philosophy, theology, and psychology. Partial or full expressions of it may be found in the works of such diverse thinkers as Plato and Kierkegaard, Aristotle and Jaspers, Augustine and Buber, Viktor Frankl and Abraham Maslow, and Thomas Aquinas and Lawrence Kohlberg.[3] One may also see them in the scriptures of Christianity, Judaism, Islam, Hinduism, and Buddhism. Throughout the last thirty-five hundred years one can see them recur again and again in the cultures of North and South, East and West. Many of us will view this theory as common sense, and after reading it, will say, "That makes a lot of sense. You've put words to what I've always known." But it is worth putting words to common sense, because it will help us to articulate the urgings of our hearts, to formulate plans for growth in purpose, to find paths to greater psychological health (and even sanity), and to make the most out of our time, talent, and lives.

The third and fourth levels of happiness (inspired by the Golden Rule) have great bearing on the philosophy in this book, for they have the capacity to transform the "mind's reasons" into the "heart's reasons".[4] When many people read the aforementioned Principles 1–9 for the first time, their *minds* are engaged. They are not only trying to understand the principles, but also are trying to survey the effects that they have had on the growth of civilization (as well as

[3] The precise citations of the works of all these thinkers may be found in ibid., pp. 59–60, notes 3–12.

[4] See Blaise Pascal, *The Pensées* (Baltimore: Penguin Books, 1961), no. 277.

the problems that arise when cultures ignore them). Yet, this engagement of the mind can allow for a curious emotional distance from the principles, as if they are something we are looking at through a window, and it is here that we may want to intentionally engage our hearts. These principles have a nobility that can stir the spirit of mankind to heights of idealism, progress, and transformation of civilization. They have moved the most influential leaders in world history to accomplishments that were not even dreamt before—accomplishments that gave rise to the protection of populations, the burgeoning of cultures, and a horizon for the common good that have led to a better life for everyone. The personal and cultural movement from a dominant Level 2 identity (comparative, ego-in) to a dominant Level 3 identity (contributive, ego-out) is the step necessary for the engagement of the heart that transforms these principles from "interesting concepts" to "noble ideals", and so these levels of happiness/identity merit deeper exploration.

As will become clear, human beings possess four kinds of desire. The fulfillment of each kind of desire leads to happiness, while the nonfulfillment of these desires leads to unhappiness. One of these kinds of desires (or happiness) will become dominant in our lives, and when it does it will become our purpose in life. As this purpose becomes habitual, it will become our dominant identity. Thus, there is a natural progression from a dominant desire (happiness) to purpose in life to identity. The four *kinds* of desire/happiness may be organized into four *levels* in accordance with the degree to which they produce effects that are pervasive, enduring, and deep. "Pervasive" means to produce effects which go further and further beyond the self; "enduring" means to last longer; and "deep" means to utilize the higher powers of human consciousness, such as intelligence, creativity, idealism, moral reasoning, love, spiritual awareness, etc. The lower levels, though more immediately gratifying, intense, and surface-apparent, are less pervasive, enduring, and deep. The higher levels are precisely the opposite.

Level 1 is the desire for externally stimulated or physical pleasures and possessions (e.g., a bowl of linguini or a new Mercedes e-Class with leather upholstery).

Level 2 is an ego-gratification arising out of shifting the locus of control from the outer world to one's inner world (*ego*, "I"). Such ego-gratifications might take the form of increases in status, admiration, achievement, power, control, winning, etc., and generally entail a comparative advantage that compels questions such as, "Who's got more intelligence; who's got less intelligence?" and "Who's got more status; who's got less status?"

Level 3 is the desire to make a difference in the world. This moves in the opposite direction of Level 2. Instead of shifting the locus of control from the outer world toward one's inner world, it invests one's inner world in the outer world, that is, it tries to make an optimal positive difference to the world (e.g., to family, friends, organization, community, church, culture, and kingdom of God) with one's time, talents, energy, indeed, one's life. It can occur through both action and empathy (being with others) and occurs most powerfully through *agape* (love without expectation of return, love for the sake of the beloved).

Level 4 is the desire for the ultimate, unconditional, or perfect in Truth, Love, Goodness, Beauty, and Being. Faith identifies perfect and unconditional Truth, Love, Goodness, Beauty, and Being with God; and so Level 4, for people of faith, is the desire for God.

The following diagram summarizes the above four levels of desire/happiness.

Normally, one of the four levels of desire becomes dominant, and the others become either recessive or ignored.

Four Levels of Desire/Happiness

Ultimate or Unconditional Purpose

4

Objective: Seek and live in ultimate Truth, Love, Goodness, Beauty, and Being (Platonic transcendentals).

Characteristics: Seeking the unconditional, unrestricted, perfect, eternal in above transcendentals. Can come from pursuit of transcendentals or faith/God/religion. Optimal pervasiveness, endurance, and depth.

Contributive (Ego-out)

3

Objective: Optimize positive difference in the world. (The world is better off for my having lived.) Comes from "doing for" and "being with".

Characteristics: More pervasive (positive effects beyond self), enduring (lasts longer), and deep (using highest creative and psychological powers). Can come from generosity, magnanimity, altruism, love.

Comparative (Ego-in)

2

Objective: Shift locus of control to self (ego) and gain comparative advantage in status, esteem, power, control, winning, and success.

Characteristics: Intense ego-gratification (sense of progress, superiority, and esteemability). If dominant, then fear of failure, ego-sensitivity, ego-blame/rage, self-pity, inferiority, suspicion, resentment.

Physical/External Stimulus

1

Objective: The pleasure or material object itself (nothing beyond this).

Characteristics: Immediate gratification, surface apparent, and intensity of stimulus. No desire for common, intrinsic, or ultimate good.

The dominant desire becomes our purpose in life (and, eventually, our personal identity), while recessive ones serve the dominant one. Ignored desires generally frustrate or debilitate us. Even though all four desires are functional, the dominant desire (or identity) tends to control the way we view success and our goals in life; the way we conduct relationships and view love, our principles and ethics, the ideals we seek; and the way we judge our self-worth, our progress in life, and our very selves. Needless to say, the kind of desire we allow *or* choose to become dominant is one of the most important decisions in our lives.

As one moves *up* the four levels of desire, one attains more pervasive, enduring, and deep purpose in life. For example, Level 3 or 4 purpose has a much greater effect in the world (more *pervasive*) than a Level 1 or 2 purpose (which is restricted to *self*-benefit). Similarly, Level 3 and 4 purpose *endures* much longer than Level 1 or 2 purpose. Level 4 purpose even endures unto eternity. Finally, Level 3 or 4 purpose is *deeper* (utilizes our higher powers of creativity, intellection, moral reasoning, love, and spiritual awareness) than Level 1 or 2 purpose. If efficacy in life is determined by the pervasiveness, endurance, and depth of one's actions, then the higher one moves up the levels of desire, the greater the effectiveness of one's life.

The only "down side" to this ascendancy of effectiveness and purpose in life is that one has to delay gratification, look beneath and beyond the surface of life, and give up some degree of intensity. It is clear that Level 1 is immediately gratifying, surface apparent, and intense, while Level 4 frequently requires nuance, education, subtlety, delay in gratification, and detachment from intensity. Thus, the higher levels are marked by a trade-off—in order to attain to universal and eternal effects arising out of our self-transcendent powers of Truth, Love, Goodness, Beauty, and Being, we frequently have to give up some degree of immediate gratification, intensity, and surface apparentness.

This "trade-off" marks one of the most difficult challenges of the identity transformation, for it is not easy to let go of what is so easily and intensely satisfying. Yet, it is worth it, for the move to Levels 3 and 4 fills us with higher purpose, more enduring (even eternal) effects, and awakens the highest, most sophisticated powers within us. Moreover,

Level 4 introduces us to the transcendent domain and the spiritual life.[5]

As noted above, each level of desire/happiness can become dominant, and when it does, it becomes our purpose in life and our identity. In other books, I explain that human beings can only be *ultimately* satisfied by a Level 4 identity, because our desire for the unconditional and perfect in Truth, Love, Goodness, Beauty, and Being can never be satiated by what is conditioned or imperfect. Inasmuch as God is unconditional and perfect Truth-Love-Goodness-Beauty, then God can satisfy us.[6]

Now let us turn to a matter of considerable significance, namely, the transition from a dominant Level 2 (comparative, ego-in) identity to a dominant Level 3 (contributive, ego-out) identity. The reason for emphasizing this transition is that it is the one with which most people in our culture will have to contend many times throughout their lives. Even though there are a large number of people who have a dominant Level 1 identity, many more people in our culture are unconsciously situated at a dominant Level 2 identity—and suffering significant emotional consequences because of it.

Recall that Level 2 is almost always linked to comparisons. In order to shift the locus of control from the outer world to the inner world, I must constantly ask myself, "Who is achieving more? Who is achieving less? Who is making more progress? Who is making less? Who is winning? Who is losing? Who has got more status? Who has got less status?

---

[5] A more detailed explanation of Level 4 and the spiritual life may be found in Spitzer, *Five Pillars*, epilogue.

[6] See Spitzer, *Healing the Culture*, chapter 3; Spitzer, *Five Pillars*, epilogue; and Spitzer, *New Proofs for the Existence of God: Contributions of Contemporary Physics and Philosophy* (Grand Rapids, Mich.: Eerdmans Publishing, 2010), chapter 8.

Who is more popular? Who is less popular? Who has got more control? Who has got less control? Who is more admired? Who is less admired? Who is more intelligent? Who is less intelligent?" Notice that one is using these comparative questions to obtain identity. Thus, one is literally living for a Level 2 answer to these questions and is therefore treating these comparative characteristics as *ends in themselves*. Hence, one is not achieving in order to contribute to family, colleagues, or the culture; one is achieving as an end in itself, as if achievement gave life meaning. Similarly, one is not seeking status in order to have the credibility to do good for others or even the kingdom of God. One is simply seeking status as an end in itself. The same holds for winning, power, control, intelligence, and so forth.

Notice further that Level 2 is not bad. Indeed, quite the opposite. The desire for achievement leads to progress in civilization. The desire for respect leads to credibility, confidence, and self respect. The desire to win leads to competitiveness and the seeking of excellence. Even the desire for power can be used for good purposes. So what's the problem? The problem is not Level 2, but living for Level 2 *as an end in itself*. When one does this, then achievement leads to compulsive "getting ahead", instead of "a good beyond the achievement". Seeking respect leads to pandering after admiration. Power sought as an end in itself corrupts—and absolute power sought in itself corrupts absolutely.

A variety of consequences follows from this narrow purpose in life: one may feel emptiness arising out of "under-living life". The desire to make a positive difference (or even an optimal positive difference) to family, friends, community, organization, colleagues, church, culture, and society (Level 3) goes unfulfilled. One begins to think that one's life doesn't really make any difference to the world or to history: "The world is not better off for my having lived."

To make matters worse, one's desire for the ultimate (in Truth, Love, Goodness, Beauty, and Being—indeed, God) is also unfulfilled. Though one may long for the ultimate with all one's heart, one's obsession with Level 2 precludes the pursuit of Levels 3 and 4. Again, one's spirit reacts with a profound sense of emptiness, a sense of underliving life, a more and more poignant awareness that "I am wasting the little precious time I have in this world."

Additional negative emotions accompany this sense of emptiness. Most of these emotions arise out of a fixation on comparative advantage. Since a dominant Level 2 identity treats status, admiration, power, control, winning, etc., as ends in themselves, it is compelled to seek comparative advantage as its fulfillment. This fixation requires not only that I progress more and more (in status, power, winning, and so forth), but also that I have *more* of it than Joe, Sue, Frank, and Mary. When I do not have more, when I am not better than others, I profoundly believe that my life is either stagnant or slipping away. I feel a profound diminishment in self-worth and success. And so I begin to feel jealousy, a malaise about life, inferiority, loneliness, frustration, and even a sense of self-pity and resentment.

One might respond that these negative emotions do not befall the dominant Level 2 *winner*, for to the victor go the spoils. While it is true that winners do receive significant ego-gratification, it is worth noting that the above-mentioned emptiness still follows in its wake. Furthermore, such winners are obliged to increase in their Level 2 successes, because they cannot attain any sense of progress without doing so. If they do not continually increase in their successes, they experience the same kinds of malaise, inferiority, jealousy, frustration, and self-pity as nonwinners.

Moreover, these winners contract a peculiar disease, namely, the desire to be overtly admired. When perceived inferiors do not acknowledge the winner's superiority (and their own inferiority by comparison), the winner feels tremendous resentment. "You have not given me the accolades I deserve. And, furthermore, you are actually treating yourself as my equal—who do you think you are?" This peculiar disease has another aspect, namely, contempt. Dominant Level 2 winners can't help it. They really do feel that their lives are worth more than other people's lives, and so they either project contempt or (if they are more enlightened) they are patronizingly condescending ("That's a nice *little* project you did there"). In the end, such winners cannot afford to fail; if they do, those whom they have treated with contempt will savage them.

Furthermore, a winner's self-image cannot tolerate being embarrassed in front of inferiors. Let us suppose you are a reasonably intelligent person, and you mispronounce the word "spectroscopy" in a public lecture, to which a colleague says, "I cannot believe that a person of your caliber would make such a mistake." You go to your room, close the door, and play that excruciating tape over and over again in your mind until you want to do yourself physical harm, for the physical pain would be so much better than ... "I can't believe I made that mistake in public!" Dominant Level 2 winners also feel the need to blame others for failures (because, in principle, they cannot fail).

In sum, winners better be perfect; but then again, they can't be altogether perfect. So winners must construct a huge façade and then protect it; but then again, they cannot construct a façade impenetrable enough to keep observant inferiors at bay. So, dominant Level 2 winners better be prepared for contempt, resentment, blame, anger, debilitating ego-sensitivities, and, above all, loneliness—for no one (except Mother Teresa, and maybe their own mothers) will want to be around them for any other reason than sheer necessity.

The reason I know all these things is because I have struggled and continue to struggle with these negative emotions (from both winning and losing). Nevertheless, I (and many others) can attest that Level 3 (contributive/love) and Level 4 (transcendent/spiritual life) help immeasurably to diminish the pain, emptiness, and obsession of a dominant Level 2 identity.

Unfortunately, making Level 3 and Level 4 a dominant identity is not as easy as simply making a choice. We have to allow ourselves to be at home with that choice and then allow that choice to become habitual, so that we do not have to think about it all the time. This requires writing down certain concrete aspects of one's new Level 3/Level 4 identity, reviewing this document every morning for at least a month, and reflectively trying to resolve the tensions and problems that arise out of living in this new identity. I have found one particular technique to be quite helpful in carrying out this reflection process: write your own personal creed.

The easiest way to proceed with this task is to write down on a single sheet of paper (two sides, if you must) the ways in which you think you can make an optimal positive difference with your particular time, talent, and energy, to the following groups, if applicable: family, friends, co-workers, stakeholders at work (employees, customers, etc.), church, the kingdom of God, your community (charities, sports teams, community boards, or other ways in which you might interact with the community), the culture (working in an educational institution, on a political campaign, or in the arts or the media where you might be able to influence people's values and ideals), and, finally, the greater society (if you are a political or cultural leader). Ask yourself, "How can my part of the world be optimally better off for my having lived?" or "How can I leave an optimal legacy to my part of the world with my time, talent, and energy?" These questions take our attention away from who has more comparative advantage (e.g., "Who is more or less intelligent?"), and instead put the focus on how we can use our intelligence, status, talents, energy, and time to make the world optimally better for our having lived. After completing this creed, conclude with the words: "For this I came." This statement makes the list more than a set of aspirations and transforms it into a life *purpose* or *identity* statement.

Remember, in order to get the most out of this exercise, once you have completed the creed, you must reflect on it for at least five minutes every day for at least a month, and you must also reflect on the tensions that this new identity may cause, particularly when it comes into conflict with the dominant Level 2 identity, with which you may be more comfortable. Be patient with yourself. You will tend to return to the dominant Level 2 identity at least twenty times per day for a long time. However, stay the course, because in my experience (as well as that of many others), slowly but surely, the new identity will begin to take hold, reversions to the former dominant Level 2 identity will happen less frequently, and a new (almost addictive) sense of purpose and spirit in life will come in its wake. Along with this new sense of purpose and spirit will come a marked decrease in the anxieties of jealousy, fear of failure, ego-sensitivities, ego-rage, blaming of others, self-pity, contempt, inferiority, superiority, and the other negative emotional conditions mentioned above. Thus, this one change in perspective can lead not only to much greater efficacy in life, but also to greater happiness.

There is another remarkable effect stemming from this identity transformation, namely, the engagement of our hearts in the nine universal principles set out earlier in this book. As noted above, the engagement of the heart transforms these principles from "interesting concepts" to "noble ideals", and this makes all the difference. If you, the reader, have chosen to move toward Level 3 or Level 4, and if that purpose in life is beginning to take a dominant position within your psyche, and if you are feeling a marked decrease in the negative emotional conditions mentioned above, you will then want to reread the first nine principles set out in this book, and you may want to consider the life issues in the light of these principles grasped through both the mind and the heart. If you resolve that these principles merit more than mere intellectual consideration, then I would ask that you teach them and take action against the obvious injustices they elucidate.

Six Categories of Cultural Discourse

We now have only one more subject to consider, namely, how to speak about these issues within the culture. There are six terms (concepts) that seem to come up not only in the discussion of the life issues, but also with any issue concerned with the ten universal principles:

1. Quality of Life/Success
2. Freedom (or "Choice")
3. Ethics/Virtue
4. Love
5. Suffering
6. Social Responsibility and the Common Good

The reader may have already surmised that the definitions of these terms change along with one's level of desire/happiness. Thus, if one has a dominant Level 1 view of desire/happiness, one will view quality of life or freedom in a very different way than if one has a dominant Level 2 or dominant Level 3 view of desire/happiness. This means that there will be at least four different meanings for each of the above six terms (concepts), which can make speaking to the culture very difficult. A person at Level 2 may say, "We must protect freedom", and this could mean something totally different from a Level 3 person's desire for freedom. Aside from the obvious miscommunications which can result, one can expect misunderstanding of motives, suspicion of others, unnecessarily heated debates, and a host of other problems opening upon a kind of cultural chaos. So what can we do about it?

At the very least, we can be certain about what *our* dominant purpose/identity is, what level of discourse we are using, and help others to clarify the level of discourse they are using. This will help to sort out unnecessary miscommunications and misunderstandings, leaving only those differences which are truly substantive. If you are a Level 3 person and seek to make the world an optimally better place for your having lived, you are going to have a very different view of the six above-mentioned terms (and the ten principles) than someone who has a dominant Level 2 identity. Unless you can convince this person to move to Level 3, you may as well agree to disagree, because your fundamental definitions of terms, your interpretation of the ten principles, and your position on the issues will simply be incongruent. However, if you disagree on the issues, first see if there is some Level 3 common ground upon which you both can stand. If there is common ground, then see if you can get a common Level 3 understanding of the six above-mentioned terms. And if you can, then you will be able to make progress about discussing and implementing the ten universal principles.

So how can we get a consistent understanding of the six above-mentioned concepts? I will here set out a brief synopsis of each, showing the changes in definition that occur according to the level of desire/happiness through which they are interpreted. If you would like a much fuller explanation of these concepts, you will want to consult my book *Healing the Culture: A Commonsense Philosophy of Happiness, Freedom, and the Life Issues* (chapters 4–7; see note 2 above on page 90). Let us begin with the concept of "quality of life".

Quality of Life/Success

It should come as no surprise that our views of quality of life and success will mirror our view of happiness/purpose; for if we are happy and have purpose, we will think of ourselves as having a good quality of life and as being successful. Therefore, our definitions will very likely fall into the following categories.

Level 1. Having a good quality of life and being successful is contingent upon acquiring many material possessions, feeling entertained, having access to sensual pleasure and kinesthetic activities (e.g., skiing), and having nice things to wear, etc.

Level 2. Factors for a high quality of life and success are having competitive advantage, having talents that will enable us to stand out and be respected; being respected by people who we respect; having status that can be objectively measured (e.g., high-prestige career, influence in public, academic qualifications); being competitive or a winner; having control or power in family, organizational, community, and societal settings; having admirers and feeling elite or special.

Level 3. A high quality of life and success is defined by having an optimal positive impact on family, friends, community, organization, colleagues, church, culture, and society; being able to leave a legacy; and having good empathetic relationships (where giving is as important as receiving). The objective is to make the best use of one's time, talent, and energy to make a positive difference rather than counting one's talents (say, intelligence) as ends in themselves.

Level 4. Having optimal quality of life and success is being able to contribute to a cause that will last for an eternity; being able to contribute to the building of the kingdom of God; having an impact on others that will last for an eternity (e.g., helping others with their faith); engaging in activities that will be pleasing to God; the pursuit of absolute Truth (theological truth); the pursuit of absolute Goodness/Justice (theological goodness); loving surrender to God; and being at home with God.

Freedom

The way we view happiness/purpose also affects the way we view freedom, because freedom can either serve us alone, or it can serve some purpose beyond ourselves, and even an ultimate purpose beyond ourselves (God). This will affect the way we view options, commitment, self-sacrifice, and surrender.

Level 1. I feel free when I am getting my strongest sensorial desires met as quickly as possible. I feel free when I can get an ice cream cone when I want it; when I can get cash from my bank account when I want it; when I can be emotionally satisfied by somebody else when I want it (e.g., get sympathy or affection). It also refers to being able to avoid emotionally dissatisfying situations as quickly as possible. I feel free when I don't have to study for an exam; when I don't have to help Joe; when I don't have to do chores. Evidently, this notion of freedom is antithetical to commitment.

Level 2. When I am in relationship with others, I feel most free when I am getting what I want over against others; when I can make my will felt; when others cannot constrain me; when I can constrain others. When I am by myself, I feel most free when I am self-determined and when I can keep all my options open for as long as I would like (avoiding commitments which would foreclose perfectly good options). If I have to be committed (select a course of action which will require time and energy, and therefore will foreclose certain options), I feel best when I am able to achieve the goals which will bring me status, admiration, power, and success. Thus, the notion of freedom accommodates some measure of commitment and self-sacrifice, but only to achieve goals which will benefit me and my long-term comparative advantage. I feel constrained (not free) when somebody else's will prevails over mine; when someone has power over me; when I have to do things for somebody else (which will not advance my ego-comparative goals); when I have to spend time with people who will not advance my long-term ego-comparative goals; or when I cannot pursue the fullest degree of competitiveness because of the ethical concerns or perceptions of others.

Level 3. I feel free when I am advancing a noble purpose that will make the world better; when I am leaving a legacy that is truly worth my time and energy; when I am entering into common cause with similarly committed people to achieve a noble purpose; and when I am able to pursue what is most pervasive, enduring, and deep without being inhibited by the need for ego-gratifications, sensorial distraction, recognition from others, and comparative advantage. This notion of freedom shifts the focus from getting what I want (Level 1) or being in control or on the top (Level 2) to actualizing what is objectively good for something or someone beyond myself. It therefore makes accommodation for, and values, the fruits of discipline, commitment, and self-sacrifice. One may find this discipline to be difficult, commitments to be tedious, and self-sacrifice to be painful, but one appreciates the ability and the freedom to do these things in order to actualize an objective good. Notice that this freedom means that one does not feel constrained (unfree) by discipline, commitment, and self-sacrifice, but precisely the opposite (i.e., free to be able to do a good that is difficult, tedious, and painful, but nonetheless worthwhile).

Level 4. Freedom is seeking the will of God and acting on it out of a conviction that God's will is what will actualize what is most pervasive, enduring, and deep. There is a willingness to commit myself and make sacrifices of what I would like, or what I would will (even if these seem to be contributive) in order to actualize what I believe to be the will of God. Therefore, this kind of freedom is frequently identified with surrender to God. The fruit of this kind of freedom is being an instrument of God; being able to do what is most pervasive, enduring, and deep in the eyes of God, which may be at odds with what I might think; and being at peace with my surrender to God, even if this requires giving up what I want (Level 1); giving up achieving a goal that would bring status or power (Level 2); or even giving up doing something that I think would be very contributive (Level 3), but which may conflict with something that I consider to be the will of God. Freedom is being at peace with, and being able to accomplish, whatever I discern to be the will of God according to his truth and his love (which may not necessarily be my view of truth or love).

Ethics/Virtue

Ethics and virtue generally arise out of Level 3 or Level 4. Dominant Level 1 and Level 2 individuals are generally not internally motivated to be ethical; they generally require some extrinsic motivation or reward.

Level 1. This group tends to embrace modern epicurean values: there is very little comprehension of ethics/virtue having value and there is no internal motivation to learn about or pursue ethics. This group is generally perplexed as to the purpose of ethics. If persons from this group believe that they will obtain a pleasure-materialistic advantage from appearing ethical, they will probably accommodate this by giving the appearance that matters of virtue and ethics are important. Otherwise, if someone is appealing to persons from this group to be ethical or virtuous for its own sake (because it's the right thing to do), these individuals will meet this suggestion with almost complete indifference.

Level 2. Inasmuch as Level 2 requires delayed gratification in order to obtain success, status, perceived intelligence, control, and power, this group tends to embrace modern stoic values (courage, perseverance, and self-discipline), because these virtues tend to manifest strength, autonomy, and competitiveness (all of which tend to help in the pursuit of Level 2 goals, image, and status). Dominant Level 2 persons often treat the virtues of courage, perseverance, and self-discipline as ends in themselves. They may pursue these virtues in order to see themselves as "above mediocrity" and even superior to others. In a dominant Level 2 perspective, these virtues do not serve higher virtues such as prudence (conscience), justice, and love, and therefore could be used in the service of arrogance, injustice, and cruelty.

Level 3. In this perspective, the "other-centered" virtues have priority over the stoic virtues. Thus, prudence (conscience), justice, or love (or all three) are seen as "end virtues" while the stoic virtues are seen as "means virtues". The stoic virtues are necessary to carry out end virtues (e.g., one must have courage and self-discipline in order to be just and loving), but the stoic virtues are not viewed as ends in themselves. In a Level 3 view, the principle of nonmaleficence is undisputed and indispensable for a good life, because the Golden Rule (Level 3) presumes the Silver Rule; and since Principles 6, 7, 8, and 9 are natural extensions of the principle of nonmaleficence, they too are viewed as undisputed and indispensable for a good life. Persons in this group tend to value and listen to conscience, and to subscribe to Principle 5 (the end does not justify the means), and therefore feel themselves accountable to some rules or ethical precepts, (such as "don't cheat", "don't lie", "don't steal"). They also tend to see the Golden Rule as a value because the Golden Rule is essentially contributive. Therefore, they see social responsibility and altruistic activity (to better mankind) as a part of their ethical obligation. They generally have a sophisticated sense of community and frequently subordinate individual goods to the common good.

Level 4. In the West, the transcendent and religious perspectives tend to hold all of the tenets of Level 3 ethics (see above). There is generally a belief that all of these tenets are part of the divine will; therefore, they have value not only because they avoid unnecessary harm to others, do good for others, and enable us to pursue our ends in the right way (for the sake of others), but also because these actions are pleasing to God, who is generally viewed as just and loving. There is the expectation that God cannot be less just or loving than any human being, and so there is little tension between Level 3 ethical objectives and Level 4 ethical objectives. This group would attest that prayer, grace, and common cause with a just and loving God reinforces and helps them in their ethical beliefs and conduct.

Love

Love (*agape*) may be defined as empathy for another leading to a unity with another whereby doing the good for the other is just as easy, if not easier, than doing the good for the self. There are other notions of love, such as feelings of affection (*storge*); friendship (*philia*), and romantic love (*eros*). *Agape* is a Level 3/Level 4 virtue, because it is essentially contributive (seeking the good for the other). Inasmuch as a dominant Level 1 seeks pleasure-materialistic satisfactions and a dominant Level 2 seeks ego-comparative satisfactions (and can even be narcissistic), these lower levels can come into conflict with *agape*. However, this group can experience the other kinds of love as specified below.

Level 1. Since dominant Level 1 individuals are likely to subordinate contributive ideals to pleasure-materialistic satisfaction, it is unlikely that they will pursue *agape*. They may not even be able to understand the value of *agape*. These individuals' experience of love generally focuses on feelings of affection (*storge*) and feelings of romantic love (*eros*); they do not generally see these feelings as serving the greater end of *agape*. These feelings tend to be ends in themselves. Persons in this group also form significant friendships (*philia*), but these friendships tend to be what Aristotle termed "friendships of pleasure", or "friendships of utility", not friendships arising out of empathy, which lead to doing the good for the other as if one were doing a good for oneself. In light of all this, it is unlikely that persons in this group will be able to understand and appreciate Principles 5–10.

They may be able to appreciate Principle 4 (nonmalefi-cence) as a necessity to maintain appropriate social order so that pleasure-materialistic satisfactions will not be interrupted.

Level 2. Dominant Level 2 individuals may experience occasional moments of empathy and may actually desire to make a positive difference in the world; but their preoccu-pation with achieving comparative, ego-in advantage tends to overshadow their positive sensibilities and motivations. When comparative, ego-in advantage becomes obsessive, it leads to narcissism, which almost completely precludes empa-thy and contributive motivations. In this respect, a domi-nant Level 2 may be less successful at *agape* than a dominant Level 1, because the dominant Level 2 could actually destroy *agape* in order to achieve comparative, ego-in satisfaction. Like the dominant Level 1, this person's experience of love focuses on feelings of affection (*storge*) and romantic feel-ings (*eros*). These feelings of *eros* can be tied to a narcissistic need *to be* loved, and persons in this group can mistakenly think that they are practicing *agape*, when in reality, they are simply appreciating the admiration or romantic love that others have for them. This is not to say that "being loved" is inconsistent with *agape*, because it is quite consistent so long as it is accompanied by genuine empathy for the other, whereby doing the good for the other is just as easy as doing the good for oneself.

Persons in this group also focus on friendships of plea-sure and utility, and on friendships of what Aristotle called "intellectual companionship" (frequently to reinforce their sense and reputation of being intelligent and elite). When the ego-comparative identity becomes obsessive, it can lead not only to narcissism, but also to elitism, which may pro-duce a subconscious contempt (and even hatred) for per-ceived inferiors. This could lead to contempt for Principles

5–10, which may be seen as elevating inferiors to an undeserved status that entitles them to undeserved rewards. This group may be quite unaware of the narcissism and elitism underlying this contempt, because they may feel that they subscribe to the "correct" positions in other important areas of justice (such as alleviating hunger or disease). If a genuine feeling of *agape* (authentic, empathetic, self-sacrificial love) truly underlies this concern for justice, then these individuals can be persuaded to move to a consistent Level 3 position of love (which would include the unborn, the elderly, the physically and mentally challenged, etc.).

Level 3. The ideal of love for these individuals is to make *agape* primary, while allowing the other three loves (*storge, eros,* and *philia*) to reinforce, enhance, and be directed by *agape* in ways that are appropriate to them. This can be very difficult to accomplish, because people do not achieve the ideal of Level 3 love in an instantaneous fashion. The process is filled with new beginnings, fits and starts, setbacks, slow progress, frustrations, and a myriad of other challenges. Thus, a person trying to move from dominant Level 2 to dominant Level 3 may be sorely tempted to be narcissistic, to place *being loved* above *loving others,* and to place romantic gratification over authentic empathy and self-gift *at the very moment* they are trying to prioritize *agape.* This mindset can be exceedingly frustrating and even discouraging. However, the pursuit of Level 3 love is worth the effort, because it eventually alerts us to our moments of inauthenticity and helps us to deepen the authenticity of *agape* in our lives. Every frustrating setback, when dealt with patiently and maturely, produces both of these beneficial effects.

Changes in external circumstances (such as being promoted, acquiring a Ph.D., gaining increases in status or financial resources) can also lead to setbacks because they can tempt individuals to bask in their new Level 2 glory and, as a consequence, move away from authentic empathy and self-gift. Once again, perseverance is the key. When one discovers oneself reverting to a dominant Level 2 view of love, one must again rekindle one's sense of the intrinsic goodness, mystery, and lovability of every individual (inducing empathy), and one's sense of nobility for making an optimal positive difference with one's life in the world. Every setback which is appropriately redressed will again produce authenticity and depth of *agape*.

When Level 3 love grows in depth and authenticity, Principles 4–10 will be viewed as self-evident, undisputed, and indispensable. It would be unthinkable and unbearable for someone with authentic empathy and contributive spirit to advocate unnecessary harm to anyone (Principle 4), to use unjust means to attain just ends (Principle 5), to value human beings as anything less than their fully developed potential (Principle 6), to deny human beings the rights that belong to them by their very nature and existence (Principle 7), to put one group's liberty or property rights above the right to live (Principle 8), and to lay undue burdens on one group in order to produce new freedoms for others (Principle 9).

Level 4. These individuals are generally motivated by a recognition that God loves them in an unconditional and perfectly authentic way. This recognition stems from their awareness of the intrinsic goodness, mystery, and lovability of others, the goodness of *agape* as the primary meaning of life, and perfect *agape* as being integral to the Creator of human nature.[7] The recognition of God's unconditional Love for these individuals generally produces a loving response from them, which tends to be reinforced by a felt awareness

[7] See Spitzer, *New Proofs*, chapters 7 and 8, where the progression of this insight into the love of God is set out.

of his presence and guiding force. A relationship with this unconditionally loving God produces a call to ever-greater authenticity and humility, which deepens Level 3 love for neighbor. Thus, Level 4 love of God deepens the practice of Level 3 love of neighbor, which, in turn, deepens the Level 4 love of God. Additionally, Level 4 love of God alerts us to an awareness that we are not the only ones who are sacred (called to perfect Love with God). Every other human being is also sacred, and therefore inestimably precious and lovable to the unconditionally loving Creator. Thus, Level 4 love of God calls Level 3 love of neighbor to perfection. It deepens authenticity and heartfelt commitment, which, in turn, makes more unthinkable and unbearable any violation of Principles 4–10.

As with Level 3 love, Level 4 love is not instantaneous. It also takes time to gain in strength and authenticity, and this process will be filled with frustrations, challenges, and setbacks. However, as with Level 3 love, every setback, dealt with patiently and maturely, can be the pathway to continued growth in *agape*.

Suffering

Giving meaning to suffering again depends on one's level of desire/happiness because this view will determine the kinds of value we will see in suffering. The benefits of suffering are generally found in Level 3 and Level 4, because suffering can help us to detach ourselves from superficial purpose in life (living beneath ourselves), to value making a positive contribution beyond ourselves, to value humility as the way to make *agape* authentic, to see the value of relationship with a loving God, and to allow God to help us in our pursuit of virtue and love. There are some Level 2 benefits of suffering that might be termed "stoic benefits". These would include becoming stronger, more courageous, and more experienced through the pains of challenge in life. The following will make this clear.

Level 1. Inasmuch as these individuals embrace modern epicurean beliefs by interpreting quality of life in terms of pleasure-materialistic satisfactions, and inasmuch as suffering can deprive them of these satisfactions, suffering is viewed very negatively. Inasmuch as the benefits of suffering are generally found in Level 3 and Level 4 (and stoic benefits in Level 2), these individuals will usually see little benefit in suffering. Hence, suffering seems to be a pure negative without any purpose. The only recourse left to these individuals is to compensate suffering with sensorial-materialistic pleasure (e.g., eat something, drink alcohol, or go shopping). Unfortunately, such pleasures have a limited value in their capacity to compensate for suffering, and so long-lasting or deep suffering will generally be viewed as unmeaningful and can very likely lead to anxiety, depression, and even thoughts of death. Many in this group would consider euthanasia to be a social good. They may also believe that abortion is a good solution for children who would be born into poverty.

Level 2. Inasmuch as individuals in this group attribute value to stoic virtues (strength, courage, self-discipline, perseverance; see above), they are likely to interpret suffering positively in light of them. The sufferings of war have value because they help to control fear and refine courage. Suffering that leads one close to death is good because "what does not kill me makes me stronger". Inasmuch as all suffering can lead to greater self-discipline, it can help to meet significant challenges more easily. Suffering can also help one rise above mediocrity and the baseness of humanity, which can be a significant ego-comparative boost.

The difficulty with this view of suffering is that it treats the stoic virtues as ends in themselves, and inasmuch as stoic virtues are self-centered, suffering has no value beyond oneself. Thus, if suffering reaches a point where it is too debilitating to be compensated by stoic benefits, these individuals will devalue themselves and their lives. Instead of moving above mediocrity, they will feel themselves slipping into mediocrity, which may lead them to anxiety, depression, and even thoughts of death. Suicide was considered noble by many classical stoics ("It is better to be dead than the living dead").

This group would tend to view euthanasia for people slipping into mediocrity as a social good. They might also tend to view aborting children who would be born without opportunity for wealth or advancement to be a social good.

Level 3. These individuals believe that there are significant benefits in suffering. They see suffering as helping to lead to identity transformation (from Level 1 to Level 2 to Level 3) and believe that their progress from superficial purpose in life to contributive-efficacious purpose comes, in many respects, from suffering. They also believe that suffering is integral to their journey toward *agape* and also to the deepening of *agape* in their lives. Many of these individuals believe that suffering leads them to greater toleration of weakness, more empathy for others, a decrease in feelings of superiority and contempt, a more realistic sense of themselves, more compassion for others in their weakness, more forgiving attitudes toward others, and other attributes integral to *agape*. If these individuals see stoic virtues arising out of suffering, they do not treat them as ends in themselves, but rather tend to see them as helping the primary virtue of *agape* ("The self-discipline and courage that comes with my suffering helps me to be a more loving person").

Since individuals in this group are alert to the possibility of identity transformation and more authentic *agape* arising out of suffering, they tend to look for these opportunities in suffering, and so help to bring them about. Thus, even though they may feel sadness, challenge, and malaise during times of extended suffering, they are less likely to become depressed and despairing (though this can happen).

This group tends to view the last months of life as very important, because great progress can be made in forgiveness, compassion, empathy, and *agape*, which not only can deepen the heart of the suffering person, but also can leave a legacy for survivors. Thus, this group tends to view euthanasia as a waste of one of the most important periods of life. Furthermore, this group does not restrict "life's opportunities" to those which would produce advancement, status, comparative advantage, power, and other Level 2 benefits, but rather sees opportunities in being contributive to family, friends, community, church, etc., and in using empathy and friendship as a way of helping others. Thus, a lack of Level 2 opportunity does not equate with meaninglessness of life, and so the abortion of children who are born into poverty (or who may lack Level 2 opportunities) is not viewed as a social good, but rather as a waste of a life that could be filled with love and be optimally contributive.

Level 4. These individuals generally believe that love (*agape*) is the meaning of suffering, and that God is Love. Therefore, they believe that God will redeem their suffering by guiding them to greater opportunities and depths of love, and that they do not have to be the primary instruments through which suffering will become efficacious. They see God guiding them to new paths of life, new opportunities to serve, new friends with whom to serve, and new communities in which to participate. These changes produce a new efficacy and sense of purpose. These individuals also see God as guiding them to eternal life. As such, although they may feel quite bereft at, say, the loss of a loved one, they do not see any particular suffering as *ultimately* tragic, because all suffering will be redeemed in God's loving eternity. In their faith, they see God as helping them to see the transcendent and eternal dignity (sacredness) of every human being, and so they are inclined to help others see this dignity in themselves. Thus, they see suffering as helping them to be disciples of both love and hope in the world.

Though these individuals can feel great sadness and loss in times of suffering, their faith tends to obviate depression and despair so long as they continue to trust in God and remember his unconditional Love. Since they view all human beings as having transcendent and eternal dignity, they see suffering as something positive and leading toward unconditional Love in eternal life. As such, they do not view euthanasia as either an individual or social good. Furthermore, since they view every individual as having a transcendent and eternal dignity, they do not see human beings as the possession of any other human being, but rather the possession of God. Therefore, they tend to view abortion in all its forms as a violation of this sacred dignity.

Social Responsibility and the Common Good

Our view of social responsibility and the common good follows directly from our views of freedom, ethics, and love. It is best to avoid associating a particular economic or political system, for example, capitalism or Marxism, with any specific level of social responsibility and common good, but rather to use the most proven principles of economics and social theory to carry out our convictions about the common good.

Level 1. Since persons in this group have an individualist-emotive view of freedom (having one's strongest desire or emotion fulfilled as soon as possible), an epicurean view of ethics (to assure enough social order to allow for uninterrupted pleasure-materialistic satisfactions), and a view of love that focuses on *storge, eros,* and limited kinds of friendship, they will not have a developed view of social responsibility or the common good. Even if they understand these concepts, they will very probably not care about them and will not factor them in to their decision-making process. Therefore, they will be unmotivated by Principles 5–10 and may not even want to learn about these principles. They will not want to involve themselves in the formation of culture and will probably consider this to be a waste of time.

Level 2. Since people in this group have an autonomous view of freedom ("I feel free when I am in control and when others are not impinging upon me"), a stoic view of virtue that values virtues such as courage and self-discipline, and a view of love that focuses on *storge, eros,* and limited kinds of friendship, they will generally limit their view of social responsibility and the common good to what they can influence and control, and to areas from which they can obtain Level 2 benefits. Therefore, they are unlikely to have an interest in domains of the common good that are outside their sphere of influence. They may be curious about Principles 5–10, but will be unlikely to promote them (or care about them) beyond their sphere of influence.

Level 3. Individuals in this group move beyond freedom as mere self-determination and see freedom as the ability (discipline and commitment) to actualize optimal contribution in the world. They also believe that stoic virtues are sub-ordinated to ends virtues, such as justice and love, and so are naturally disposed toward the common good considered in itself (not the common good within one's sphere of influ-ence). This group also views love in terms of authentic *agape*, and so feels not only a responsibility for, but also a compas-sion toward all human beings, particularly those who are marginalized or in need. As one grows in Level 3 commit-ment (see above, Love, Level 3), one develops a deeper sense of social responsibility and takes action to help both neigh-bor and stranger. Inasmuch as Principles 4–10 are integral to the most basic concept of the common good, this group will be motivated to teach and promote these principles in all domains of culture, and to actualize these principles with respect to every relevant ethical issue.

Level 4. These individuals will have convictions similar to those in the Level 3 group. Since they believe in a tran-scendent Principle (God), they will see all human beings as belonging to God's family. They will be solid in their con-viction that Principles 4–9 should be shared with the entire world. Since they believe not only in the intrinsic value of human life, but also in the transcendent and eternal (sacred) value of human life, they will generally view Principles 4–10 as having not only a natural significance, but also a tran-scendent and eternal significance.

CONCLUSION

As can be seen, one's level of happiness and purpose in life is quite relevant to what one believes about quality of life, freedom, ethics, love, suffering, and social responsibility; and what one believes about these six concepts is quite relevant to how one values Principles 4–10. Even if dominant Level 1 and dominant Level 2 individuals understand these principles and the importance they have enjoyed in world history, they will find these principles difficult to care about or promote because they are focused on a different dimension of identity and life.

Our culture tends to foster dominant Level 2 individuals. Even though this dominant identity may make us unhappy (because of jealously, fear of failure, ego-sensitivity, etc.), we can become almost obsessed by it if we do not see it as the root of our unhappiness. As a result, we can find ourselves empty and unhappy, underliving our lives, and caring little for anything beyond "how I measure up". When this becomes one's dominant perspective, the ten universal principles seem to be little else than interesting abstractions or footnotes to intellectual history.

But if we can break free of the grip of dominant Level 2, if we can see our way clear to choosing a Level 3/Level 4 identity, if we can select some friends or groups who will help us to maintain and grow in this new identity, and if we can keep ourselves on the road to greater actualization of Level 3/Level 4 identity (despite the many setbacks that will occur), then our lives will begin to be free of the negative emotions mentioned above, begin to become more effica-cious, and begin to create a lasting legacy of Goodness and Love (even an eternal legacy). The ten universal principles will then take on a significance in our minds and hearts that they never had before, and they will become something worth protecting and even fighting for. At this juncture, the life issues will not simply be a matter of personal choice; they will be a matter of protecting the innocent and protecting our culture, and, therefore, worthy of the personal sacrifices that may be asked of us.

APPENDIX

Evidence of the Transmateriality
of Human Beings

In the discussion of the principle of nonmaleficence (section 4.B), it was asserted that human beings have an awareness of and desire for five transcendentals: *perfect and unconditional* Truth, Love, Goodness (Justice), Beauty, and Being (Home). The following is a brief explication of this assertion, which explains why human consciousness is distinct from animal consciousness, why humans have creative capacity beyond preset rules, algorithms, and programs (Gödel's proof), and why human beings have a natural propensity toward the spiritual and transcendent.[1]

I. The Desire for Perfect and Unconditional Truth

In his famous work *Insight: A Study of Human Understanding*,[2] Bernard Lonergan presents an argument substantiating the existence of our desire for (and awareness of) perfect

[1] A more thorough treatment of the following sections is given in Robert Spitzer, S.J., *New Proofs for the Existence of God: Contributions of Contemporary Physics and Philosophy* (Grand Rapids, Mich.: Eerdmans Publishing, 2010), chapters 7 and 8.

[2] Bernard Lonergan, *Collected Works of Bernard Lonergan*, vol. 3, *Insight: A Study of Human Understanding*, ed. Frederick E. Crowe and Robert M. Doran (Toronto: University of Toronto Press, 1992).

and unconditional Truth, which he terms "complete intelligibility". The argument may be set out in seven steps:

(1)   Lonergan begins with the frequently experienced phenomenon of asking further questions immediately upon arriving at answers. We may remember our childhood when we besieged our parents with questions such as, "Why is this?" And our parents would respond, "Oh, because of that", and we would immediately ask, "Well, why is *that*?" And they would respond with yet another answer, to which we would ask another question. This ability continuously to ask questions reveals our awareness that an answer is incomplete, that is, that the answer is not *completely* intelligible, that it does not explain "everything about everything". If we did not know that an answer was incompletely intelligible, we would not ask any further questions. We would be very content to know our names and to respond to biological opportunities and dangers—nothing more. It is the awareness of "something more to be known" at the very moment when something is known that drives the further question.

(2)   Lonergan affirms that he has a pure *unrestricted* desire to know, that is, he desires to know *all* that is to be known, and that he has the capacity to ask further questions when he has not yet grasped "all that is to be known".

(3)   Now, the question arises: how could I have the power to ask a question every time I understand something that does not meet the expectation of "all that is to be known"? It would seem that I would have to have some awareness (at least a tacit awareness) of "all that is to be known" sufficient to know that whatever I have grasped has not yet met this objective. Thus, I

might move from analytical geometry, to calculus, to non-Euclidian geometries, to the tensor, and know that the tensor does not adequately describe the whole of mathematical intelligibility—and it truly does not. Similarly, I can attain an understanding of space-time fields, electromagnetic fields, quantum fields, the grand unified field, etc., and realize that the grand unified field still does not exhaust all that is to be known— and it truly does not. This applies to every area of inquiry and every field of knowledge, and I would know if my idea did not *explain everything about everything.*

(4)   The question again arises: how would I always know that there is more to be known when I have grasped even the highest ideas through the highest viewpoints? How would I know that those ideas and viewpoints did not explain everything about everything? How do I know what qualifies for an explanation of everything about everything? How can I have a "preknowledge" (an awareness) of the explanation of everything about everything sufficient to keep on asking questions, and to know what will fail to meet the objective of an explanation of everything about everything? This last question presents an essential clue to our transcendentality. How would I be able continuously to recognize incomplete intelligibility (even in the highest and most grandiose ideas) if I did not have some tacit awareness of those ideas failing to qualify for *complete* intelligibility? Wouldn't I have to have some sense of what complete intelligibility is in order to recognize the limits of the intelligibility of the idea I have already grasped? Doesn't the recognition of a limit mean that I have to be beyond the limit? If I weren't beyond the limit, how could I recognize it to be a limit? A limit of what?

Therefore, it seems that I must have a tacit awareness of "what is sufficient to qualify for an explanation
of everything about everything". Obviously, I cannot
explicitly know all the *contents* that I do not know; but
I could have a *tacit* awareness of what would be sufficient for an explanation of everything about everything. This would explain how I could reach very high
viewpoints of mathematics, physics, and metaphysics,
and still know that I did not have an explanation of
everything about everything—and even have a sense
of where to turn to find such an explanation.

(5) What could be the origin of this awareness? It cannot
be a physical or restricted source (empirical data, finite
data, or the contents of restricted acts of understanding) because the tacit awareness of "what is sufficient
for an explanation of everything about everything" is
always *beyond* every "intelligible reality *that leaves a question unanswered*", and every *restricted* intelligible always
leaves a question unanswered: Why?

Any restricted intelligible must leave a question
unanswered because the intelligibility (information) available to answer questions about it is restricted. Thus,
there can always be more questions about a restricted
reality than there will be intelligibility (information
within the restricted reality) available to answer them.
Why? Inasmuch as the *answers* from a restricted intelligible have an intrinsic limit (i.e., they do not keep on
going indefinitely), they will eventually be open to further questions that cannot be answered by the restricted
intelligible itself. Thus, we might say that every restricted
intelligible is *more* questionable than answerable. There
will always be a domain of answers that give rise to
more questions than the intelligibility of the restricted
reality can answer. Therefore, the tacit awareness of "what

is sufficient for an explanation of everything about everything" is always beyond any *restricted* intelligible.

Therefore, the source of this "tacit awareness that is always beyond restricted intelligibility" must be *unrestricted* intelligibility. Lonergan asks himself what unrestricted intelligibility could be. He knows it cannot be a physical reality, because the intelligibility of physical reality is restricted by space, time, and other algorithmically finite structures. He therefore settles upon a transphysical or transmaterial reality, such as an unrestricted idea (within an unrestricted act of understanding). Needless to say, such an unrestricted act of understanding cannot be viewed as a brain, which is material and restricted by space, time, and other algorithmically finite structures; so Lonergan refers to it as a "spiritual" reality. This spiritual reality—this unrestricted act of understanding, which is the ground of the idea of unrestricted intelligibility—would seem to be the source of my tacit awareness of "what is sufficient for an explanation of everything about everything".

(6) Even though the idea of complete intelligibility is the *source* of my tacit awareness of "what is sufficient for an explanation of everything about everything", I cannot say that I *understand* this idea, because it must be grounded in an *unrestricted* act of understanding, which I, evidently, do not have.

But how can this be? Lonergan uses the terminology of "notion"—"the notion of being", or, what I would term, "the notion of complete intelligibility". What is a notion? It is a presence to consciousness— not a presence that is held or controlled by my consciousness, but one that is held or controlled outside of my consciousness while still being present to it. Now if I do not understand this presence, then how am I aware of it? I must be aware of it as something on the *horizon*, as something beyond my understanding, but, nevertheless, something which can act as a *backdrop* over against which I compare the ideas which I *have* understood. This would explain how I would know that there is more to be known at the very moment I have understood something new and would explain how I would know that the tensor is not the complete explanation of mathematics, and that mathematics is not the complete explanation of intelligibility itself. I am comparing it to a backdrop that is so much more than the highest possible viewpoints, so much more than any restricted intelligible, so much more than any content of a *restricted* act of understanding.[3]

Now, as I said, I do not understand, hold, or control this idea; it is, as it were, held and controlled for me as a backdrop to compare the intelligibility of the ideas that I *have* understood. But what is holding and controlling this idea for me as a backdrop? I must adduce that it would be its source, namely, the unrestricted act of understanding.

(7)   This would mean that the idea of complete intelligibility, that is, the content of an unrestricted act of understanding, the divine essence, is present to me as a horizon, that is, as a backdrop that can be compared to every intelligible content I grasp through my

---

[3] Lonergan expresses it as follows: "[T]he notion of being penetrates all cognitional contents. It is the supreme heuristic notion. Prior to every content, it is the notion of the to-be-known through that content. As each content emerges, the 'to-be-known through that content' passes without residue into the 'known through that content.' Some blank in universal anticipation is filled in, not merely to end that element of anticipation, but also to make the filler a part of the anticipated. Hence, prior to all answers, the notion of being is the notion of the totality to be known through all answers" (ibid., pp. 380–81).

restricted acts of understanding. The presence of the divine essence, therefore, must be the impetus for my awareness of incomplete intelligibility, the impetus for every question, the impetus for every act of creativity.

If the divine essence were not present to me, I would only be capable of recognizing objects of biological opportunity and danger, such as food, snakes, my name, affection, etc., but nothing more, for I would not ask questions about intelligibility, such as what, why, and how, which penetrate the nature of reality. My curiosity would be limited to biological opportunities and dangers, to discerning the mood of my master, to detecting whether an herb smells right, or a creature is dangerous. Intelligibility—the nature of things, heuristic contexts, the what, why, and how—would be quite beyond me, totally unrecognized by me. Therefore, I would not have a *pure* desire to understand, let alone a pure, *unrestricted* desire to understand. Without the notion of complete intelligibility—the presence of the idea of complete intelligibility (the presence of the divine essence)—I would find fulfillment through a fine piece of meat and ignore the tensor.

The above argument for the existence of our transcendental awareness of complete intelligibility, and the presence of its transphysical, unrestricted source to our consciousness, is remarkably probative. Regrettably, the cost we must pay for this probative force is the nuance and complexity of the argument. The reader will be relieved to know that the other arguments for the existence of our desire for perfect and unconditional Love, Goodness (Justice), Beauty, and Being (Home) are less nuanced and complex, but consequently have less probative force. Perhaps it is best for the reader to use the above argument as a foundation for and a light through which to see the other four transcendental desires, which express the fullness of our communion with their transphysical source.

II. The Desire for Perfect and Unconditional Love

Human beings also appear to have a "sense" of *perfect and unconditional Love*. Not only do we have the power to love, i.e., the power to be naturally connected to another human being in profound empathy, emotion, care, self-gift, concern, and acceptance, we have a "sense" of what this profound interpersonal connection would be like if it were perfect. This sense of perfect Love has the positive effect of inciting us to pursue ever more perfect forms of Love. However, it has the drawback of inciting us to *expect* ever more perfect Love from other human beings. This generally leads to frustrated expectations of others and consequently to a decline of relationships that can never grow fast enough to match this expectation of perfect and unconditional Love.

This phenomenon gradually manifests itself. For example, as the first signs of imperfection, conditionedness, and finitude begin to emerge in one's beloved, one may show slight irritation, but have hopes that the ideal will soon be recaptured—as if it were ever captured to begin with. But as the fallibility of the beloved begins to be more acutely manifest (the other is not perfectly humble, gentle, kind, forgiving, self-giving, and concerned with me in all my interests) the irritation becomes frustration, which, in turn, becomes dashed expectation: "I can't believe I thought she was really the One." Of course, she wasn't the One, because she is not perfect and unconditioned. Nevertheless, the dashed expectation becomes either quiet hurt or overt demands, both aimed at extracting a higher level of performance from the beloved. When the beloved does not comply, thoughts of terminating the relationship may arise.

The root problem was not with the authenticity of this couple's love for one another. It did not arise out of a lack of concern, care, and responsiveness, or a lack of desire to be self-giving, responsible, self-disciplined, and true. Rather, it arose out of a false expectation that *they* could be *perfect* and *unconditional* Truth, Love, Goodness (Justice), Beauty, and Being (Home) for one another.

Why do we fall prey to what seems to be such an obvious error? Because our *desire* for love and to love is unconditional, but our *actuality* is conditioned. Our desire is for the perfect, but our actuality is imperfect. We, as human beings, therefore, cannot satisfy one another's desire for the unconditional and the perfect. If we do not have a *real* unconditional and perfect being to satisfy this desire, we start looking around us to find a surrogate. Other human beings at first seem like a very good surrogate, because they display qualities of self-transcendence. Hence, we confuse one another for the perfect and unconditioned, and undermine the very relationships which hold out opportunities for growth, depth, joy, common cause, and mutual bondedness.

What is the origin of this desire for unconditional Love? Just as the unrestricted desire to know must include a notional awareness of complete intelligibility to give rise to an awareness of and dissatisfaction with every manifestation of incomplete intelligibility, so also the desire for unconditional Love must include a notional awareness of unconditional Love to give rise to the awareness of and dissatisfaction with every manifestation of conditioned and imperfect Love. This notional awareness of unconditional Love seems to be beyond any specifically known or concretely experienced love, for it seems to cause dissatisfaction with every conditioned love we have known or experienced. Thus, our dissatisfaction would seem to arise out of an ideal of unconditional Love, which has neither been experienced nor actualized. How can we have an awareness of love that we have neither known nor experienced? How can we even extrapolate to it if we do not know where we are going? The inability to give a logical answer to these questions has led some philosophers to associate the desire for unconditional Love with "the notion of unconditional Love within us", which would seem to have its origin in unconditional Love itself.

Lonergan believes that when we fulfill our desire for unconditional Love by authentically loving God, we simultaneously fulfill our capacity for self-transcendence, which includes our desire for perfect Truth, Love, Goodness, Beauty, and Being: "I have conceived being in love with God as an ultimate fulfillment of man's capacity for self-transcendence; and this view of religion is sustained when God is conceived as the supreme fulfillment of the transcendental notions, as supreme intelligence, truth, reality, righteousness, goodness." [4]

Once again, the human awareness of and desire for the perfect and unconditional manifests a dimension which is not reducible to algorithmically finite (physical) structures; and so it seems that we have yet another transphysical (spiritual), self-transcendent power.

III. The Desire for Perfect and Unconditional Goodness (Justice)

As with the "sense" of perfect and unconditional Truth and Love, philosophers have long recognized the human desire

---

[4] Bernard Lonergan, *Method in Theology* (New York: Herder and Herder, 1972), p. 111.

for perfect Goodness (Justice). Not only do human beings have a sense of good and evil, a capacity for moral reflection, a profoundly negative felt awareness of cooperation with evil (guilt), and a profoundly positive felt awareness of cooperation with goodness (nobility); they also have a "sense" of what perfect, unconditioned Goodness (Justice) would be like. Human beings are not content simply to act in accordance with their conscience now; they are constantly striving for ways to achieve the more noble, the greater good, the higher ideal. They even go so far as to pursue the perfectly good or just order.

A clue to this desire for perfect Goodness (Justice) may be gleaned from children. An imperfect manifestation of justice from parents will get the immediate retort "That's not fair!" Adults do the same thing. We have a sense of what perfect Goodness (Justice) ought to be, and we believe others ought to know this. When this sense of perfect Goodness (Justice) has been violated, we are likely to respond with outrage. A violation of this sort always seems particularly acute. We seem to be in a state of shock. We really expect that perfect Goodness (Justice) ought to happen, and when it does not, it so profoundly disappoints us that it can consume us. We can feel the same outrage toward groups, social structures, and even God.

One need only look at last year's newspapers to find a host of well-meaning, dedicated, and generous men and women who have tried to extract the perfect and unconditioned from the legal system, the ideals of social justice, and institutions dedicated to the common good. The despairing rhetoric of dashed idealism and cynicism does not belong solely to early Marxism; it can be found in public defenders who decry the legal system for prosecuting the innocent, and victims who vilify the very same system for letting the guilty go free. It can also be found in educators who criticize the educational system for not setting high enough standards, and in community advocates who tear down the very same system for making the standards too high and too exclusive. But our imperfect world will not allow either side to be *perfectly* correct.

As with our "sense" of perfect and unconditional Love, our sense of perfect and unconditional Goodness (Justice) has both a positive and negative side. The positive side is its ability to fuel all our strivings for an ever more perfect social order, a more just legal system, greater equity and equality, and even our promethean idealism to bring the Justice of God to earth. The negative side of this "sense" of perfect or unconditional Justice is that it incites our expectations for *perfect* Justice in a *finite* and conditioned world, meaning that our promethean ideals are likely to be frustrated. This causes disappointments with the culture, the legal system, our organizations, and even our families. We seem to always expect more Justice and Goodness than the finite world can deliver, and it causes outrage, impatience, judgment of others, and even cynicism when it does not come to pass.

What is the source of this "sense" (notion) of perfect Goodness (Justice), even the promethean desire to save the world, and to be the "ultimate hero"? As with the desire for complete intelligibility and unconditional Love, the desire for perfect Goodness (Justice) seems to go beyond any experience or knowledge of justice we could possibly have. Our frustrated idealism reveals that we continually see the limits of any current manifestation of goodness and justice, which, in turn, reveals that we are already beyond those limits. Given that our desire will only be satisfied when we reach perfect, unconditional Goodness (Justice), it would seem that our desire is guided by a notional awareness of perfect, unconditional Goodness (Justice); and, given that this notion cannot be obtained from a conditioned and imperfect world, it would seem that its origin is from perfect, unconditional Goodness (Justice) itself. For this reason, philosophers have associated it with the presence of God to human consciousness. This presence of perfect and unconditional Goodness (Justice) to human consciousness further reveals the transmaterial (spiritual), self-transcendent dimension of human beings.

IV. The Desire for Perfect and Unconditional Beauty

One need not read the nineteenth-century Romantic poets or listen to the great Romantic composers or view the works of Romantic artists to see the human capacity to idolize beauty. One only need look at the examples of simple dissatisfaction with beauty in our everyday lives. We do not look good enough and neither do other people. The house is not perfect enough, the painting can never achieve perfection, and the musical composition, though beautiful beyond belief, could always be better. Once in a great while, we think we have arrived at consummate beauty. This might occur while looking at a scene of natural beauty—a sunset over the water, majestic green and brown mountains against a horizon of blue sky—but even there, despite our desire to elevate it to the quasi divine, we get bored and strive for a different or an even more perfect manifestation of natural beauty—a *little* better sunset; another vantage point of the Alps that's a *little* more perfect.

As with the desire for the other three transcendentals—perfect Truth, perfect Love, and perfect Goodness (Justice)—human beings seem to have an awareness of what is more beautiful. It incites them to the desire for this more perfect ideal. This desire has both a positive and a negative effect. The positive effect is that it incites the continuous human striving for artistic, musical, and literary perfection. We do not passively desire to create; we passionately desire to create, to express in ever more beautiful forms the perfection of beauty that we seem to carry within our consciousness. We do not simply want to *say* an idea; we want to express it beautifully, indeed, more beautifully, and, indeed, perfectly beautifully. We do not simply want to express a mood in music; we want to express it perfectly beautifully. This striving has left a legacy of architecture and art, music and drama, and every form of high culture.

The negative effect is that we will always grow bored or frustrated with any imperfect manifestation of beauty. This causes us to try to make perfectly beautiful what is imperfect by nature. It is true that a garden can achieve a certain perfection of beauty, but our continuous desire to improve it can make us grow terribly dissatisfied when we cannot perfect it indefinitely.

This is evidenced quite strongly in the artistic community. When one reads the biographies of great artists, musicians, and poets, one senses the tragedy with which art is frequently imbued. What causes these extraordinarily gifted men and women to abuse themselves, to judge themselves so harshly, so totally to pour themselves into their art? Perhaps it's when art becomes a "god", when one tries to extract perfect and unconditional Beauty from imperfect and conditioned minds and forms.

Where does this sense of perfect Beauty come from? As with the other three yearnings for the ultimate, we are led to the beautiful itself, for dissatisfaction with even the most beautiful objects of our experience reveals our ability to perceive indefinitely the limits of worldly beauty, which, in turn, reveals our ability to be beyond those limits and reveals a notional awareness of what perfect Beauty might be (a notional awareness of a beauty without imperfection or limit). Therefore it is not surprising to see the divine associated with perfect Beauty and also with majesty, splendor, magnificence, grandeur, and glory.

This notional presence of perfect and unconditional Beauty to human consciousness further reveals the transmaterial (spiritual), self-transcendent dimension of human beings.

V. The Desire for Perfect and Unconditional Being (Home)

Human beings also seek a perfect sense of harmony with all that is. They not only want to be at home in a particular environment; they want to be at home with the totality, at home in the cosmos. This is confirmed by Mircea Eliade's exhaustive study of world religions,[5] which may be summarized as follows. Religion is grounded almost universally in a sense of the sacred, which is not reducible to a mere subjective projection. Rather, the sacred is a source or cause of human striving to live in a spiritual and transcendent domain. This domain is not a sterile concept, but rather is filled with transcendent awareness and emotion frequently resembling what Rudolf Otto terms the sense of "creatureliness", "*mysterium tremendum*", "awesomeness", "overpoweringness" (or "majesty"), "energy" (or "urgency"), "fascination", and "transcendent otherness".[6]

---

[5] Mircea Eliade, ed., *The Encyclopedia of Religion*, 16 vols. (New York: Collier Macmillan, 1987).

[6] See Rudolf Otto, *The Idea of the Holy: An Inquiry into the Non-Rational Factor in the Idea of the Divine and Its Relation to the Rational* (New York: Oxford University Press, 1958), chapters 3–6.

Exhaustive as Eliade's (and others') studies are, it is important to validate this conclusion for ourselves. Have you ever felt, either as a child or an adult, a sense of alienation or discord, a deep sense of not belonging? You ask yourself, "What could be the source?" and you look around and see that at this particular time you have a good relationship with your friends and your family. Your work relationships seem to be going fairly well; community involvements have produced some interesting friends and contexts in which to work. Yet, something is missing; you do not quite feel at home in a *general* sense. Yet you do feel at home with family, friends, and co-workers. You feel like you are out of kilter with, and do not belong to, the *totality*. And yet, all the *specific* contexts you look at seem just fine. You feel an emptiness, a lack of peace, yet there seems to be no reason as to why you feel this way.

Many philosophers and theologians connect this feeling with a human being's yearning to be at home with the totality—not merely at home with myself, my family, my friends, or even the world, but to be perfectly at home (without any hint of alienation). When the desire for perfect Home is even partially fulfilled, philosophers, theologians, and mystics variously refer to it as joy–love–awe–unity–holiness–quiet.

What is the origin of our desire to be at home with all that is, to live in what Eliade termed the "sacred domain"? What gives us the capacity to experience what seems to be transcendent joy–love–awe–unity–holiness–quiet? Indeed, what enables us to sense transcendent otherness and to be able to bridge the gap between ourselves and this transcendent Other? Does not the transcendent Other have to bridge the gap to us? If so, then our sense of perfect and unconditional Home further reveals our connection and participation with a transmaterial (spiritual), self-transcendent domain.

Conclusion

If we examine our own desires and capacities in the domains of Truth, Love, Goodness (Justice), Beauty, and Being (Home), it is difficult to deny the presence of transmaterial awareness and desire, which seems to indicate a connection with a transmaterial source of that desire. This connection, in turn, reveals the transmaterial dimension of human beings.

If we wish to reduce humanity to mere materiality, to mere artificial intelligence, and to mere animalist consciousness, we will not only have to ignore Gödel's proof for non-reductionistic human intelligence; we will also have to equate ourselves with beings that lapse into sleep without the stimulus of biological opportunities and dangers. More than this, we will have to deny the presence of all the above transcendental desires within ourselves, desires that cannot be explained through algorithmically finite, physical structures. This seems a rather high price to pay, for it would mean condemning ourselves to ignore everything that matters—Truth, Love, Goodness (Justice), Beauty, Being (Home)—at its highest possible level. Do we really want to do this, all for the cause of defending materialism or justifying serious violations of the principle of nonmaleficence? It would seem to be complete self-negation in the effort to negate the true dignity of every human being. This is probably not the best way to make the most of our lives.

BIBLIOGRAPHY

Published Books and Articles

Aquinas, Thomas. *Summa Theologica*. Translated by Fathers of the English Dominican Province. New York: Benziger Brothers, 1948.

Aristotle. *Aristotle's Metaphysics*. Translated by Hippocrates G. Apostle. Grinnell, Iowa: Peripatetic Press, 1979.

———. *Posterior Analytics*. Translated by Jonathan Barnes. New York: Oxford University Press, 1994.

———. *Prior Analytics*. Translated by Robin Smith. Indianapolis: Hackett Publishing, 1989.

Augustine. *On Free Choice of the Will*. Translated by Thomas Williams. Indianapolis: Hackett Publishing, 1993.

———. *Treatise against Lying (Contra Mendacium)*. Chicago: Adams Press, 1979.

Barnhart, Robert K. *Chambers Dictionary of Etymology*. New York: H. W. Wilson, 1988.

Barr, Stephen M. *Modern Physics and Ancient Faith*. Notre Dame: University of Notre Dame Press, 2003.

Black's Law Dictionary. 5th ed. St. Paul: West Publishing, 1979.

Blackstone, William. *Commentaries on the Law: From the Abridged Edition of Wm. Hardcastle Browne*. Washington, D.C.: Washington Law Book, 1941.

Collins, Francis. "Collins: Why This Scientist Believes in God". *CNN.com*, April 3, 2007. http://www.cnn.com/2007/US/04/03/collins.commentary/index.html.2007.

Eddington, Arthur. *The Nature of the Physical World*. Cambridge: Cambridge University Press, 1928.

Eliade, Mircea, ed. *The Encyclopedia of Religion*. 16 vols. New York: Collier Macmillan, 1987.

Finnis, John. *Natural Law and Natural Rights*. New York: Oxford University Press, 1980.

Foley, Kathleen. "The Relationship of Pain and Symptom Management to Patient Requests for Physician-Assisted Suicide". *Journal of Pain and Symptom Management* 6 (1991: 289–97).

Foley, Kathleen and Herbert Hendin, eds. *The Case against Assisted Suicide: For the Right to End-of-Life Care*. Baltimore: Johns Hopkins University Press, 2002.

Gödel, Kurt. "Über formal unentscheidbare Sätze der Principia Mathematica und verwandter Systeme I". *Monatshefte für Mathematik und Physik* 38 (1931): 173–98.

Hamilton, Alexander, John Jay, and James Madison. *The Federalist Papers*. McLean edition. Library of Congress, etext by Project Gutenberg, 1788. http://thomas.loc.gov/home/histdox/fedpaper.txt.

Kubler-Ross, Elizabeth. *On Death and Dying*. New York: Scribner Classics, 1997.

Las Casas, Bartolomé de. *In Defense of the Indians: The Defense of the Most Reverend Lord, Don Fray Bartolomé de las Casas, of the Order of Preachers, Late Bishop of Chiapa, against the Persecutors and Slanderers of the Peoples of the New World Discovered across the Seas*. Translated and edited by Stafford Poole. DeKalb: Northern Illinois University Press, 1992.

Locke, John. *Second Treatise on Government*. Edited by C. B. Macpherson. Indianapolis: Hackett Publishing, 1980.

Lonergan, Bernard. *Collected Works of Bernard Lonergan*. Vol. 3, *Insight: A Study of Human Understanding*. Edited by Frederick E. Crowe and Robert M. Doran. Toronto: University of Toronto Press, 1992.

———. *The Lonergan Reader*. Edited by Mark Morelli and Elizabeth Morelli. Toronto: University of Toronto Press, 1997.

———. *Method in Theology*. New York: Herder and Herder, 1972.

Lucas, John R. "Minds, Machines, and Gödel". *Philosophy* 36 (1961): 112–27.

Martin, Michael M., Daniel J. Capra, and Faust F. Rossi. *New York Evidence Handbook: Rules, Theory, and Practice*. 2nd ed. New York: Aspen Publishers, 2003.

Montesquieu, Baron de. *The Spirit of the Laws*. New York: Hafner Publishing, 1949.

Otto, Rudolf. *The Idea of the Holy: An Inquiry into the Non-Rational Factor in the Idea of the Divine and Its Relation to the Rational*. New York: Oxford University Press, 1958.

Paine, Thomas. *The Rights of Man*. Stilwell, Kans.: Digireads.com Publishing, 2007.

Pascal, Blaise. *The Pensées*. Baltimore: Penguin Books, 1961.

Penrose, Roger. *The Emperor's New Mind*. Oxford: Oxford University Press, 1989.

Plato. *Republic of Plato*. Translated by Benjamin Jowett. New York: World Publishing, 1946.

Skinner, B. F. *Beyond Freedom and Dignity*. Indianapolis: Hackett Publishing, 2002.

Spitzer, Robert J., S.J. *Five Pillars of the Spiritual Life*. San Francisco: Ignatius Press, 2008.

_____. *Healing the Culture: A Commonsense Philosophy of Happiness, Freedom, and the Life Issues*. San Francisco: Ignatius Press, 2000.

_____. *New Proofs for the Existence of God: Contributions of Contemporary Physics and Philosophy*. Grand Rapids, Mich.: Eerdmans Publishing, 2010.

Suarez, Francisco. *De Legibus*. Madrid: Consejo Superior de Investigaciones Cientificas, Instituto Francisco de Vitoria, 1971.

Thoreau, Henry David. *On the Duty of Civil Disobedience*. London: Simple Life Press, 1903.

Tierney, Brian. *The Idea of Natural Rights: Studies on Natural Rights, Natural Law, and Church Law, 1150–1625*. Atlanta: Scholars Press, 1997.

Tuckness, A. "Locke's Political Philosophy". *Stanford Encyclopedia of Philosophy Online*. Fall 2010 ed. http://plato.stanford.edu/entries/locke-political.

Tully, J. *A Discourse on Property: John Locke and His Adversaries*. New York: Cambridge University Press, 1980.

United Nations. The Universal Declaration of Human Rights. December 10, 1948. www.un.org/en/documents/udhr/index.shtml.

Court Cases

U.S. Supreme Court

Dred Scott v. Sanford, [1] 60 U.S. (How. 19) 393 (1857).
Planned Parenthood v. Casey, 505 U.S. 833 (1992).
Roe v. Wade, 410 U.S. 113, (1973), Sec. IX.B.

U.S. District Court

Simmons v. Howard University, 323 F. Supp. 529 (District of Columbia D.C. 1971).

State Supreme Courts

Davis v. Davis, 842 S.W. 2d 588, 597 (Tenn. Sup. Ct. 1992).
New Jersey v. Alexander Loce (N.J. Sup. Ct. 1991).
Raleigh Fitkin-Paul Morgan Memorial Hospital v. Anderson (N.J. Sup. Ct. 1964).
Tucker v. Howard Carmichael & Sons, 208 Ga. 201, 65 Se. 2d 909 (Ga. Sup. Ct. 1951).
Weaks v. Mounter, 88 Nev. 118, 493 P. 2d 1307, 1309 (Nev. Sup. Ct. 1972).

CONTACT INFORMATION FOR AFFILIATED GROUPS

If you have interest in obtaining more materials or helping to build a culture of life, you may want to consult the following groups. Their updated contact information may be found on their websites.

Healing the Culture

This organization is devoted to teaching the principles in this book to adult and young adult audiences. They have also designed a curriculum to teach these principles in a simplified and accessible way to high school and junior high school students. They provide teacher and facilitator training, leader manuals, written materials, and a variety of multimedia and electronic resources.

Contact information and additional resources are available on their website: http://www.healingtheculture.com.

Magis Center of Reason and Faith

This institute is devoted to making the latest information on the connection between faith and reason available to seminarians and clergy, Catholic university campus ministries, Newman Centers (on non-Catholic university campuses), high schools, and adult education programs. It has web-based curricula on (1) the astrophysical response to atheism, (2) the philosophical response to atheism, (3) the historical evidence of Jesus, and (4) suffering and the love of God. Books, written materials for students, and high school teacher training are available along with the web-based curriculum. Additional curricula will be developed for college/adult audiences in the future, including a curriculum on the contents of this book.

For data on how to view these curricula and how to obtain written materials, and for contact information, see their website: http://www.magisreasonfaith.org.

University Faculty for Life

This institute, composed of university faculty throughout the world, is devoted to academic reflection and research on the life issues. They assess not only the philosophical and political principles underlying the life issues, but also matters of biology, genetics, biochemistry, law, sociology, theology, psychology, education, and twenty-two other disciplines. Since 1990 it has published eighteen proceedings with papers and articles in these areas.

To obtain the proceedings and for contact information, see their website: http://www.uffl.org.

INDEX

a posteriori and a priori
   evidence, 14–15, 16, 76
abortion. *See* life issues
actualization and actualizability,
   17–18, 31–32, 42–43, 45n17,
   79
Aenesidemus, 6n2
agape, 10, 93, 110–14, 116–17,
   120
American Indians, 33, 45–46, 47,
   79
Aristotle
   ethics, principles of, 34
   on friendship, 110, 111
   on happiness, 91
   justice and natural rights,
      principles of, 53
   reason, principles of, 1, 5–7, 9,
      11, 12
Augustine, Saint
   consistent ends and means,
      principle of, 2, 40
   on happiness, 91
   on intrinsic value of persons, 34
   justice and natural rights, prin-
      ciples of, 71, 72n23, 73n29
Averroes, 34

beauty, desire for perfect and
   unconditional, 135–37
behaviorism, 10n4
being or home, desire for perfect
   and unconditional, 137–38

beneficence, principle of (Golden
   Rule), 3, 22, 88–91, 109
Bernton, Hal, 84n39
Bergson, Henri, 34
Beyond Freedom and Dignity
   (Skinner), 10n4
Bill of Rights, U.S., 55–56
*Blackstone Commentaries on the
   Laws of England*, 28, 29n3, 30
Buber, Martin, 91
Burke, Edmund, 72, 74

Capra, Daniel J., 69n21
checks and balances, principle of,
   82
civil disobedience and unjust law,
   71–74
Civil War, U.S., 62
Collins, Francis, 35–36
common good/social responsibility, as category of cultural discourse, 118–20
Communism, 5
complete explanation, principle
   of, 1, 8, 9–11
condition necessary for the
   possibility of _____, 75–76
consistency of evidence. *See*
   noncontradiction, principle of
consistent ends and means,
   principle of, 2, 21, 40–44
Constantine (Roman Emperor),
   90

147